MUMMIES
DEATH AND THE AFTERLIFE IN ANCIENT EGYPT
TREASURES FROM THE BRITISH MUSEUM

CATALOGUE WRITTEN BY
JOHN H. TAYLOR AND NIGEL C. STRUDWICK
CURATORS
DEPARTMENT OF ANCIENT EGYPT AND SUDAN
THE BRITISH MUSEUM
LONDON

FOREWORD BY
PETER C. KELLER
PRESIDENT
THE BOWERS MUSEUM OF CULTURAL ART
SANTA ANA, CALIFORNIA

MESSAGE BY
NEIL MACGREGOR
DIRECTOR
THE BRITISH MUSEUM
LONDON

PRESENTED BY
THE BOWERS MUSEUM OF CULTURAL ART

Exhibition organized by:
The British Museum
London

Presented by:
The Bowers Museum of Cultural Art
Santa Ana, California

Catalogue made possible by:
Resources Global Professionals
Costa Mesa, California

Additional Funding Provided by:
Parker S. Kennedy
Chairman of the Board and
Chief Executive Officer
The First American Corporation
Santa Ana, California

Printed and bound by:
P. Chan & Edward, Inc.
Korea

Design and composition by:
ThinkDesign
Buellton, California

Edited by:
Vickie C. Byrd
Executive Vice President
The Bowers Museum of Cultural Art
Santa Ana, California

ACKNOWLEDGMENTS

We would like to thank everyone who has been involved in the preparation of the objects for their journey to and display in the Bowers Museum. Vivian Davies, keeper of the Department of Ancient Egypt and Sudan in the British Museum, initiated this project and has wholeheartedly supported all of our work on it. We are grateful to all our Museum Assistants in the Department of Ancient Egypt and Sudan for their hard work, in particular Evan York, and to Claire Messenger and Tania Watkins for administering and processing the loan; important information has also been supplied by Marcel Marée, Sue Davies, and Stephen Quirke. The objects in the exhibition, coming as they do from the reserve or study collection, have needed much time and trouble to prepare them for travel, which work has been undertaken by Anne Brodrick, Helene Delauney, Francesca Harris, Michelle Hercules, Barbara Wills, Nicola Newman, Ruth Scott, and Fleur Shearman, all of the Department of Conservation, Documentation and Science. The excellent photographs in this catalogue are the work of the Photography and Imaging Department, and we thank Ivor Kerslake and Sandra Marshall for their efforts and attention to detail. Lastly we much appreciate the patience and persistence of Vickie Byrd in seeing this catalogue through to its completion.

Nigel C. Strudwick and John H. Taylor
Assistant Keepers
Department of Ancient Egypt and Sudan
The British Museum

FOREWORD

Mummies: Death and the Afterlife in Ancient Egypt…Treasures from the British Museum is the largest exhibition of mummies and related material ever to be exhibited by the British Museum outside of its own walls. The Bowers Museum is very proud to be hosting this historic exhibition as the only U.S. venue. As such, under our Joint Venture Agreement, Mummies will remain at the Bowers for as long as five years. It is very unusual in the museum community to have such an important exhibition on loan to another institution for such an extended period of time. This opportunity is due largely to the close relationship that has developed between the staff of the two institutions, as Mummies is the third exhibit after Egyptian Treasures and Queen of Sheba to be shown at the Bowers from the British Museum in just five years.

The exhibition curators, John Taylor and Nigel Strudwick, have devoted their energies to this exhibition for over two years. They have drawn upon their collection material that is well known to Egyptian scholars, and as a result have been widely published, and exhibited. However, it is very exciting that the development of this exhibition has allowed them to reach further into their vast collection and "rediscover" many items that have never before been exhibited and/or published. Some of these exciting pieces include Coffin of Seni (EA 30842), with its wonderful painted decoration; Mummy of Irthorru (EA 20745), recently splendidly restored; Massive Sarcophagus of Pakap (EA 1384); little known Statue of an Official of the late Middle Kingdom (EA 57354); and exquisite small glass inlays (EA 64642).

No exhibition of this magnitude is ever possible without an enthusiastic team of dedicated individuals. Neil MacGregor, director of the British Museum, saw the importance of the historic Joint Venture between his great institution and the Bowers Museum, which ultimately led to this exhibition. Vivian Davies, keeper, Department of Ancient Egypt and Sudan supported this exhibition from its very earliest concept stages through to its completion. John Taylor and Nigel Strudwick have put endless hours into both the exhibition and the catalogue text that you see here.

At the Bowers Museum, our Director of Exhibit Design & Fabrication, Paul Johnson, has done what he is known for which is simply stunning exhibits. Nancy Ravenhall-Johnson, our graphics designer, applied her amazing talents to produce the exquisite exhibition graphics and supporting printed materials. Vickie Byrd, executive vice president of the Bowers, worked incredible hours to assure that this catalogue is the best ever produced by the Bowers Museum, and she made certain that all the administrative aspects of this exhibition were as close to perfect as possible. Alice Bryant, the registrar for the Bowers, ensured that the exhibition was shipped and unpacked flawlessly.

Funding for this exhibition came from a variety of sources.

Peter C. Keller, Ph.D.
President
The Bowers Museum of Cultural Art

Detail from EA 1384
SARCOPHAGUS LID OF PAKAP
Section 3, Mummification

MESSAGE

The art and culture of Ancient Egypt exerts a fascination over museum visitors around the world. Much of this fascination can be attributed to the astonishing quantity of impressive objects which have survived from this ancient culture. A major aspect of the appeal of this society is the apparent obsession with death, which seems to strike a chord with our own concerns and worries about the future. Yet although this bond of humanity brings the Egyptians very near to us, many aspects of their beliefs and customs continue to captivate and intrigue us.

This exhibit presents over 130 objects arranged in seven sections to illustrate all aspects of the approach the Ancient Egyptians took towards death. While there can be no denying these people devoted an enormous amount of resources to planning for burial and the afterlife, the aim was to be well-prepared, and the Ancient Egyptians enjoyed life as much as other ancient or modern peoples.

The British Museum holds the largest collection of ancient Egyptian objects outside Egypt. The objects forming this long-term exhibit come from the study collections of the Department of Ancient Egypt and Sudan. They range from monumental expressions of the triumph over death, such as the colossal sarcophagus lid of Pakap, to small, intricately crafted items of jewelry and glassware, reflecting the more human dimension of everyday life. The majority of these objects have not been exhibited for many years, and very few of them have previously received the attention it has been possible to give them in the present exhibition. The British Museum is committed to making its collections available to the widest possible public through national and international exhibitions and displays, and the Museum is pleased to have collaborated with the Bowers Museum on this important exhibition.

Neil MacGregor
Director
The British Museum

Detail from EA 21809
MUMMY OF A CHILD WITH PAINTED PORTRAIT
Section 3, Mummification

CONTENTS

1

THE GODS

Egyptian gods are a very complex manifestation of early ideas about the divine. They were one of the many aspects of Egypt in the later 1st millennium *bc* which exercised a fascination for the Greek historians who were discovering the land for the first time. It is not difficult to imagine the impression Egypt must have made on these men who arrived there from a land where the deities were shown as humans, even though they had supra-human power: entering an Egyptian temple and being surrounded by the bewildering mixture of animals and men must have made the Greeks realize that in some way they were entering a belief system very different from their own.

Egyptian concepts of god were variable and flexible. Gods could take many different forms, even though we tend to associate one specific mode of representation with a particular divinity. Perhaps the most convincing explanation for the variety of forms which such a being could take is that the Egyptians viewed their gods as incredibly complex; representing a deity in different ways enabled them to emphasize particular aspects of the personality or the power of the god. This explains the mixture of animal and human forms that are used for many of the members of the Egyptian pantheon: the non-human inhabitants of the world had many admirable features and at times dangerous powers, and by depicting divine beings as partially or wholly in the form of an animal, that beneficence or danger could be turned to their advantage as it became part of the deity. An extreme example of the number of forms a god could possess is the sun god, always among the most important of deities. In simple terms, he could be referred to as Khepri in the morning, Re at midday, and Atum in the evening, yet in all he possessed no fewer than seventy-five forms. Other deities tend to be shown in a narrower range of manifestations, but even here variation occurred. The necropolis and embalmer god Anubis appears most often as a man with a jackal head or as a recumbent jackal, but there is at least one image of him (in the temple of Ramesses II at Abydos) in fully human form. In addition, the Egyptians were great proponents of the practice of *syncretism,* whereby aspects of two or more divinities could be merged together to produce another, which could be more powerful than the sum of the parts. Examples of this are Amun-Re (merging the state solar god with the original local god of Thebes who had risen to prominence by his devotees controlling the country), or Ptah-Sokar-Osiris, a funerary deity merging an originally Memphite necropolis deity (Sokar) with the god of the Memphite region (Ptah) and the god of the dead (Osiris).

The worlds of the living, the dead and the divine were much closer to each other in the minds of the Egyptians than they are to most inhabitants of Europe and North America at the beginning of the 21st century *ad*. The religious beliefs of the ancient Egyptians manifest themselves in perhaps three main forms—state religion, private religion, and the beliefs surrounding death—and each sphere does not impinge on the other as much as we might think. The state religion which was practiced in the major temples dedicated to the gods all over Egypt was largely a contract between the king and the gods. Various rituals had to be carried out on a daily basis to feed, worship and propitiate these deities, by which the concept of *Maat*, itself personified as a female deity, was maintained. Maat was a complex concept, but can be thought of as the world in its conventionally and correctly ordered state, with a balance maintained between king and gods, good and evil, and right and wrong. The king himself was in theory the only person who could undertake the temple rituals, and it is he who is always shown in the relief decoration as performing these acts. However, because of the number of gods and shrines it was physically impossible for him to do this on a daily basis, and so the priests of each cult deputized for him. The king would obviously attend certain major festivals and officiate there. Ordinary people had very limited access to the temples—perhaps to some of the outer courts—and they would primarily come into contact with the god through, in general terms, the overwhelming presence of the temple complex in their city reminding them of the power of god and king, and then specifically at certain festivals when the image of the god in a shrine would be carried beyond his "home" and out to visit other shrines. This is perhaps best known at Thebes where, for example, Amun-Re would travel from Karnak to the temple of Luxor, or when he would visit the Theban West Bank in festivals such as the "Beautiful festival of the Valley." Sometimes petitions were presented to gods for them to make oracular pronouncements at festivals like this.

The range of gods with specific state temples was wide, sometimes even at more than one site, but other major deities had no one state cult place and could be worshipped in a number of temples. Thus gods Geb and Nut (earth and sky) had no one major cult center. A further range of divinities appear in the popular religion of the people. For sure, they would revere some of the state deities, as shown on their stelae and tombs (see below), but in their houses and local village temples other gods are found. Some were particular local deities, such as the goddess Meretseger at Thebes or the deified king Amenhotep I, while others had no particular cult center and were concerned with basic matters of human survival. Perhaps the two best examples of the latter are Bes, the grotesque lion-maned dwarf, and Taweret, the pregnant hippopotamus. They protected the deceased while asleep, ensured human fertility and aided childbirth, to touch on just a minimal part of their functions. Small images of theses deities might be kept in the home, or even painted onto walls, to obtain their protection.

Aspects of funerary religion will be covered elsewhere in this catalogue, but in terms of the gods, it naturally involved those most concerned with aspects of death and rebirth into new life. Principal among these was Osiris, the god of the dead *par excellence,* and also Anubis, the embalmer god. Osiris, as the archetypal king of Egypt who was murdered by his brother Seth and then magically brought back to life by his spouse Isis, represented above all else the hopes of men for further life after death, and he appears in texts and images throughout this exhibition. Anubis oversaw the process of mummification, and also helped to ensure the well-being of the deceased in the cemetery. The Four Sons of Horus, represented here by a set of inlays, were part of the group of deities who oversaw the tribunal in which the dead were judged, and were specifically associated with protecting the individual internal organs removed and embalmed during the mummification process. The divine was everywhere and all-pervasive in death and life, much closer than it seems to many people today.

Literature:
Hart, *Dictionary of Egyptian Gods and Goddesses*
Hornung, *Conceptions of God in Ancient Egypt*
Wilkinson, *The Complete Gods and Goddesses of Ancient Egypt*

STATUE OF ISIS PROTECTING OSIRIS

EA 1162

Grey siltstone

Probably from Karnak

26th Dynasty, around 590 bc

Height 81.30 cm; Width 17.00 cm;

Depth 47.00 cm

Acquired in 1895

Literature: Graefe, *Untersuchungen zur Verwaltung und Geschichte der Institution der Gottesgemahlin*, 219–21, (P20), Taf. 8*, 16b, 17; see Porter and Moss, II 2nd ed. 289.

This small yet impressive statue shows a standing figure of Isis protecting with her wings a small figure of Osiris. The goddess wears a *modius*, a crown of uraeus serpents, on top of which is a pair of cows' horns and a sun-disc. The latter is worn by many female deities, and it is usually only other iconographical details and texts which permit us to identify the particular goddess. Osiris is, as usual, shown as a mummy wrapped in a tight robe, wearing the crown with the two feathers known by its Egyptian name *atef* and carrying a crook and flail, the symbols of kingship. Hieroglyphs before the feet of Osiris give the god's name and epithets and the name of the dedicator of the object; in front of those hieroglyphs is a short recitation by Isis indicating that she protects her brother and defeats his enemies. The longer text running around the base of the statue is a prayer offered up by the dedicator, Sheshonq, to Isis, requesting, among other things, a long life and a good burial.

The statue is thought to come from one of two chapels which were dedicated to forms of Osiris worshipped at Karnak. These chapels were built and extended by the adoratrices of Amun and the kings with whom they were associated (see Section 6, Furnishing of the Tomb, Object EA 68868 for more about Sheshonq).

STATUES OF SEKHMET

EA 84

EA 45

Granodiorite From Thebes

18th Dynasty, reign of Amenhotep III

Height 198.00 cm; Width 48.70 cm; Thickness 43.00 cm

Height 183.00 cm; Width 44.00 cm; Thickness 39.50 cm

Acquired from the collection of Henry Salt in 1823

Literature: Porter and Moss, II 2nd ed. 265. Yoyotte, *Bulletin de la société française d'Egyptologie* 87–88, 47–75; Bryan in Quirke (ed.), *The temple in Ancient Egypt*, 57–81.

These standing statues of the goddess Sekhmet are but two of a much larger number which originally were set up in Thebes. They show the goddess as a woman with the head of a lioness but a divine female wig. On her head is a solar disc with a *uraeus* cobra on her brow. In her left hand she holds a scepter with a top in the shape of a papyrus umbel (a *wadj* scepter); while in her right hand she holds an *ankh* sign (the hieroglyph meaning life).

Seated and standing statues of the lioness-headed goddess Sekhmet are a common sight in major museums. The largest single group of examples outside Egypt is in the British Museum, where there are in excess of thirty such statues, complete or broken. Most of them were recovered from the temple of Mut at Karnak, where many are still visible. But their original provenance was without doubt the mortuary temple of Amenhotep III on the West Bank at Thebes. Amenhotep's temple fell into decay around one hundred years after his death, and was used as a convenient quarry by many later pharaohs. Reliefs from the walls were reused in the nearby temple of Merenptah, and considerable numbers of the Sekhmet statues were moved to the Mut temple, and some kings added their names to the statues in their new locations. The association between Sekhmet and Mut is probably to be sought in the form of the lioness common to the iconography of both deities. In addition, most of the statues were positioned near the sacred lake in the temple. This lake has an unusual kidney shape, and there are other places in Egypt in which rituals to Sekhmet were carried out near similarly shaped lakes.

Statues of Sekhmet exist in seated and standing poses, and there is considerable variation between examples in the same attitude. Some are much larger than others, and the carving of, for example, the faces, suggests that they were not all produced by the same group of craftsmen—hardly surprising in view of the number produced. Some statues were carved with integral sun-discs on the head, but for many of them the sun-disc was added as a separate piece of stone which fitted into a socket at the top of the head. Although many were left uninscribed, those with inscriptions mention a variety of epithets of the goddess.

Texts in temples of the Graeco-Roman period speak of a ritual to propitiate Sekhmet, as a goddess who could otherwise be extremely dangerous; one example of her threatening aspect was her assuming the form of the Eye of (the sun god) Re. *Wadj* scepters feature prominently in these texts and accompanying scenes, and many of the epithets found on the statues echo those in the texts. One text speaks of seven hundred and thirty Sekhmets following the king, and it is possible that in the temple of Amenhotep III at Thebes there were three hundred and sixty-five standing and three hundred and sixty-five seated figures of the goddess. These could have formed a litany in stone to propitiate her permanently, lest she act with the negative power of which she was capable, thereby affecting the king and through him, Egypt. These litanies might just be associated only with the New Year, but there is also evidence that they could be celebrated in association with any momentous event. In the context of the mortuary temple, there may have been a connection with the *sed* (jubilee) festival or also Amenhotep's eternal cult.

UPPER PART OF A STATUE OF OSIRIS

EA 1667

Granodiorite

Provenance unknown

Ptolemaic Period, 305-30 bc

Height 57.00 cm; Width 35.00 cm; Depth 25.00 cm

Acquired in 1918

Literature: *Art and Afterlife in Ancient Egypt*, No. 46.

This fragment, representing the head and upper body of Osiris, probably formed part of a standing statue of the deity. The god is dressed in the usual enveloping and close-fitting robe, and holds his arms crossed on his chest; in his fists are the symbols of kingship, the crook and the flail. On his chin is the conventional divine beard, the end of which is broken off. He wears the *atef* crown, which resembled the white crown of Upper Egypt, with a feather on both sides, and a pair of ram's horns jutting out at the base. In artistic depictions this crown is most frequently worn by Osiris, although it can be shown with other gods and appears on the head of the king at times; its associations are with rebirth and renewal.

On the back pillar are the beginnings of two columns of incised hieroglyphs. Both texts are based around the formula "an offering which the king gives;" the left one is dedicated to Osiris, and the right to Isis. The name of each god is accompanied by a number of epithets, such as "foremost of the Westerners" and "lord of eternity" for Osiris, and "mother of the god" and "mistress of the two lands" for Isis. The texts break off at the point where the benefits which they are asked to give are specified, well before the name of the dedicator of the statue would have appeared.

Anubis is the Egyptian god most closely associated with cemeteries and the process of embalming. His characteristic animal is the jackal, and he is most frequently depicted as a recumbent jackal as here, or as a man with the head of a jackal. As jackals can often be found rooting around in cemetery areas, the Egyptians logically linked them with their gods concerned with matters in the necropolis; another deity more narrowly associated with burial grounds, Wepwawet, was also shown in the form of this creature.

Anubis is frequently referred to in offering prayers, and is among the relatively small group of deities who feature in tomb decoration, gods who are intimately concerned with the well-being of the dead. It is he who brings the deceased into the judgment scene in the *Book of the Dead* and/or attends the scales used in weighing the heart. Like many important state deities, he had no one principal cult center but appears frequently with other gods.

This type of wooden figure almost certainly comes from a coffin. Around 750 *bc*, there was a return in burial customs to using an exterior coffin shaped like a box, inside which were placed the anthropoid coffins or mummy-cases which contained the body itself. These new outer coffins have a vaulted roof, representing the sky, and are known by Egyptologists as *qersu* coffins; the word *qersu* ("burial" and associated words) is usually written with a

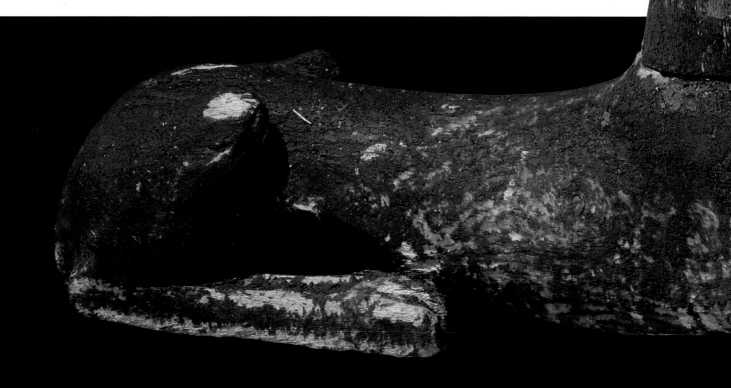

hieroglyph of a coffin with a rounded top. Wooden jackals and falcons were placed on top of these coffins as additional protection for the mummy within. Smaller wooden jackals are also found on canopic chests when production of these resumes in the Late Period, but this example is too large to come from anything but a coffin.

Like most Egyptian wooden sculpture, the jackal is made from several pieces of wood glued together. The head is made separately, as is the muzzle; in some examples the hind legs are also separate, but that does not appear to be the case here. The use of several different pieces of wood is probably not to be ascribed to the craftsman's inability to carve a single piece, but rather, to the custom of making use of every scrap of wood in a country where wood was not in extensive supply. Around the neck is a red band, probably not a decorative collar, but rather, reminiscent of the strip of cloth or leather—known as a *stola*—shown round the neck of Anubis in tomb paintings of the New Kingdom. The line of the eye and internal detail in the ears is painted yellow.

RECUMBENT JACKAL

EA 35831

Wood

Provenance unknown

Probably 25th or 26th Dynasty or later

Height 23.50 cm; Length 43.00 cm

Unpublished

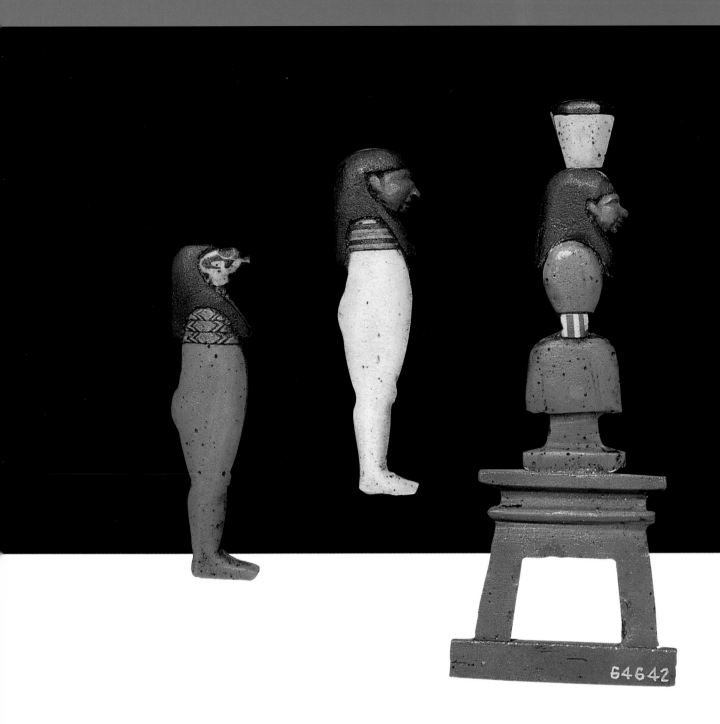

A GROUP OF AMULETIC INLAYS

EA 64642

Glass

Provenance unknown

Perhaps 1st-2nd centuries ad

Length 5.00 cm (Qebehsenuef)

Length 5.20 cm (Imsety)

Length 5.50 cm (Hapy)

Length 6.00 cm (Duamutef)

Length 9.00 cm (figures of Canopus)

Donated by Marion Whiteford Acworth in 1946, ex collection Dr. Joseph John Acworth

Literature: Cooney, *Glass*, 13 (123). Articles on glass inlays: Bianchi, *Journal of Glass Studies* 25 (1983), 29–35 and *Bulletin of the Egyptological Seminar of New York* 5 (1983), 9–29. The latter article includes as fig. 6 the cartonnage referred to at the end of this entry.

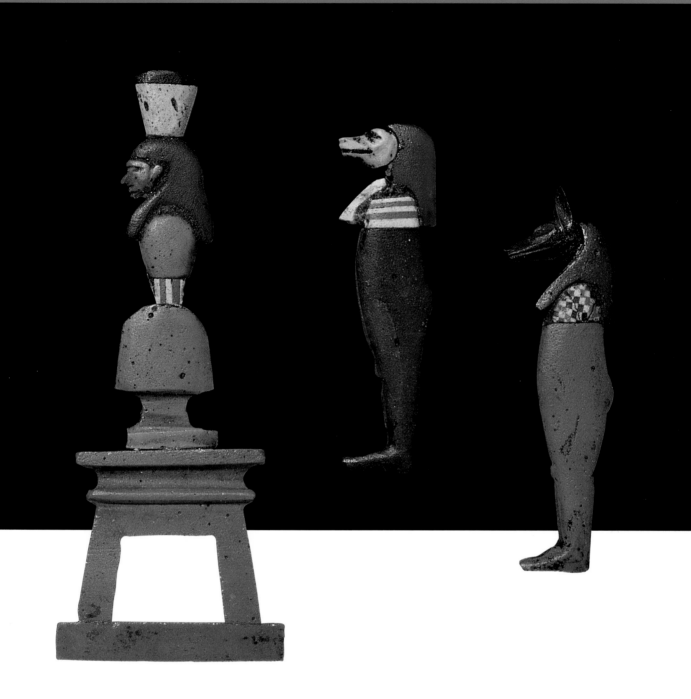

This entry consists of six polychrome glass inlay-elements in the form of deities: the standing figures represent the Four Sons of Horus who were believed to protect the deceased, and are perhaps best known from their association with canopic jars: Qebehsenuef (typically with a falcon head), Imsety (human head), Hapy (baboon head), and Duamutef (jackal head). The other two inlays show a base on which is a jar with a human head, on top of which is what appears to be a crown. This deity, not commonly represented in non-classically influenced Egyptian art, is Canopus. Canopus was a city in the Delta, where it is said that a jar-shaped local variant of Osiris was worshipped; other classical writers linked this city and its vase deity with Canopus, the pilot of the classical hero Menelaos.

From their symmetrical composition, it is likely that these inlays were intended to be set into something, most likely a piece of funerary equipment, to judge from the presence of the Sons of Horus. One possibility is that such inlays could have been used in the decoration of a cartonnage mummy-case of the Graeco-Roman Period, as at that time pieces of glass appear in masks and cartonnages as decoration; cartonnage apparently forms a good base for inlaid glass. The best example is a cartonnage which has only been viewed briefly on the art market: on this were glass inlays of the Sons of Horus and a scene of the king being baptized (see Bianchi article 2). The appearance of such inlays is probably to be traced back to the employment of small figures of the Sons of Horus on mummies and bead nets of the late Third Intermediate Period and later.

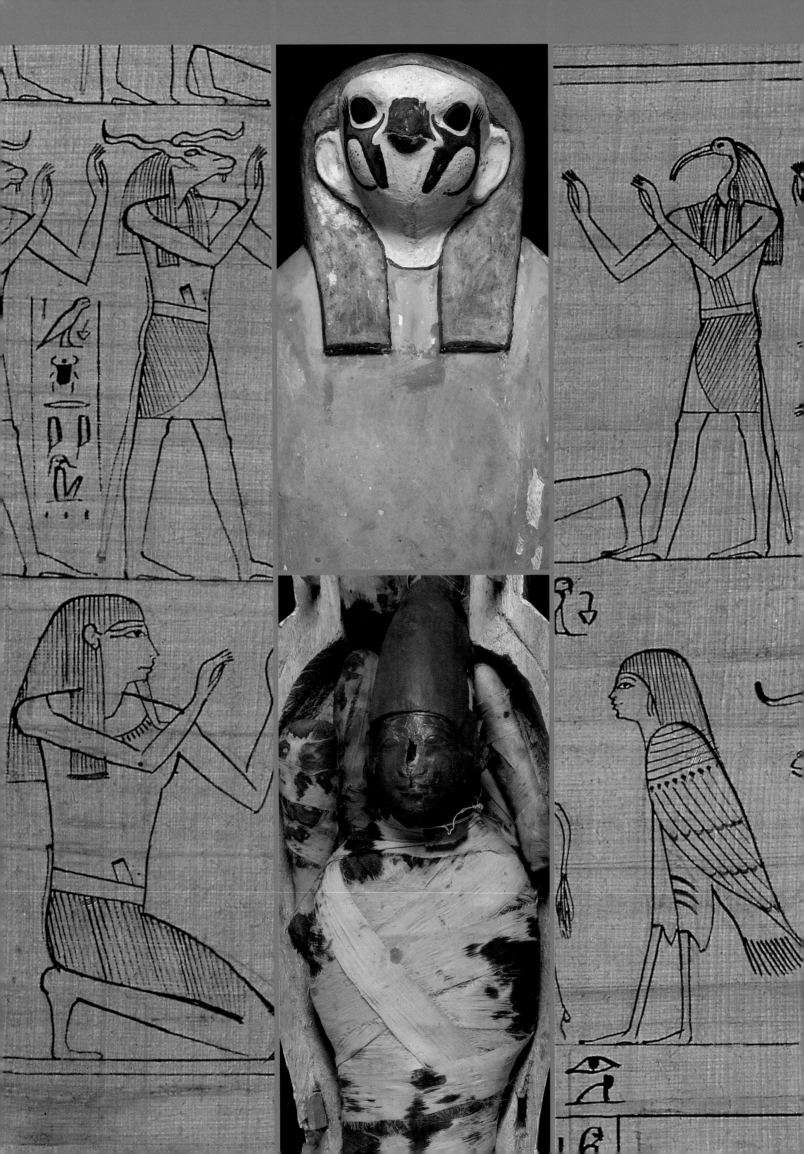

2

Beliefs About the

Afterlife

The lives of the ancient Egyptians were closely conditioned by the phenomena they observed in the universe around them: the motions of the sun, moon and stars, the annual flooding of the Nile, the cycle of vegetation. These gave promise that the world as they knew it would continue eternally. Human existence, as an inseparable part of this great scheme of creation, was also regarded as a cycle which would repeat itself for ever. The Egyptians saw the course of human life as a series of transformations. Birth, adolescence, old age and death were parts of this sequence, but, as many ancient texts make clear, death was not the end; it was merely one more transformation, leading on to another phase of existence—an eternal one. In their writings the Egyptians often likened death to a sleep or a journey, or—most significantly—to rebirth. This did not eliminate the fear and abhorrence of death any more than religious faith does in today's societies, but the Egyptians found comfort in the notion that it was a necessary preliminary to the afterlife.

The origins of the Egyptians' beliefs in an afterlife lie far back in prehistory. Graves of the earliest period (before 3000 *bc*) contained simple gifts for the dead, such as food, drink, clothing, tools and weapons—signs that at first the afterlife was regarded as being much like the earthly existence. But, with the passage of time, and the growing sophistication of Egyptian culture after 3000 *bc*, the nature of life after death came to be enshrined in a mythological framework. Because of the long evolution of the Egyptians' beliefs and their multi-faceted nature, there is no single text which explains all their notions concisely and consistently; any modern interpretation must be incomplete and subjective, but a few key points can be emphasized.

Man was regarded as a complex being that could exist both before and after death in different manifestations, known as *kheperu*. The physical body was one of these modes of existence, as were also the heart, the shadow and the name (which embodied a person's distinct identity). But even more important for the afterlife were the non-physical entities called the *ka* and the *ba*. The *ka*, in life a kind of spiritual counterpart to the individual, took on special importance after death as it was the form in which the dead received nourishment. The funerary offerings presented at the tomb were regularly described as being "for the *ka*." The *ba* could eat, drink, speak and move by itself; indeed the power of free movement was one of its chief characteristics, and for this reason it was depicted as a human-headed bird. However, none of these spiritual aspects could survive for eternity without a physical "base." In order to be nourished the *ka* had to reside either in the mummy, or in an image placed in the tomb (the *ka*-statue), while the *ba* had to be periodically reunited with the mummy if the deceased's afterlife were to continue. Rebirth, then, depended very much on the ability to restore and maintain the connection between these entities—especially that between the mummified corpse and the *ba*. Much of the ritual surrounding death and burial was devoted to bringing this about.

THE MYTHOLOGICAL FRAMEWORK:

Over the centuries the Egyptians evolved several different concepts of human survival after death. These ideas were first formulated to ensure safe passage for the dead king into the hereafter, but over time persons of lower status were able to share in the same destiny. Common to all of the concepts was the idea that resurrection was achieved through integrating the deceased into the natural processes of the cosmos. In the age of the pyramids the king was believed to ascend to the sky and dwell among the stars, but in later centuries this idea was increasingly overshadowed by other myths. In these, the creative power which brought renewal of life was associated with the gods Osiris and Re respectively.

The myth of Osiris was one of the most potent stories in ancient Egyptian tradition. Reputed to have been the model of good kingship in the remote past, Osiris was nevertheless murdered by his jealous brother Seth. His body was dismembered and the parts scattered, but Isis the sister and wife of Osiris gathered up the pieces. They were reunited and bound together in wrappings by the embalmer-god Anubis, and Osiris was restored to life to become ruler of the netherworld, the realm of the dead, while his son Horus ascended the throne on earth. Although mummification originated in Egypt centuries before this myth was first written down, the story provided a rationale for the artificial preservation of the corpse, and from the Middle Kingdom onwards Osiris was represented in mummy-form. By his example, Osiris offered the promise of resurrection after death, and therefore in the rites of burial the dead person was assimilated to the god and was regularly referred to as "the Osiris X."

The sun god Re, in contrast, was the creator of the world and all life. Although he did not suffer the violent end of Osiris, he did experience a symbolic death each evening when the sun sank below the western horizon. During the night the god made a difficult journey through the underworld, battling the forces of chaos which constantly sought to overthrow the cosmic order (*Maat*). When he emerged victorious as the rising sun in the east the god had undergone a mysterious rebirth. The New Kingdom *Books of the Netherworld*, which describe this nocturnal journey, explain that in the night the spirit of the sun god met his own corpse (equated with Osiris). This joining of the two chief manifestations of the divine being produced new life and ensured that the life-cycle of both gods would be repeated. It was a neat way of uniting two different myths, and the meeting of Re and Osiris could also be seen as the divine model for the joining of the mortal *ba* and mummy.

The ultimate goal of the deceased was to enter the divine realm, equipped with the attributes of the creator gods. This exalted state was called *akh*, a word which has connotations of luminosity and the possession of creative power. To reach this state, many preconditions had to be fulfilled: proper treatment of the corpse (including mummification), the creation of a permanent resting-place (the tomb) with a setting for the cult of the dead (tomb-chapel or royal memorial temple), and the establishment and maintenance of a funerary cult. When all these things were done, the dead person became assimilated with Osiris and Re, and could enter the afterlife. The importance that was attached to these concerns led to the investment of huge resources in the creation of the monuments and objects that were deemed essential. These are the material remains that we marvel at today—the pyramids, the painted tomb chapels, the gold trappings of the mummies, the inscribed papyri.

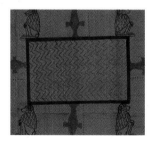

Texts do not agree about the physical location of the world of the dead or about what they would experience there. The netherworld was often referred to in metaphorical terms, which allude to aspects of death without providing a coherent description. Hence the land of the dead was "the West," because this was the place where the sun set; but it was also "the horizon" from which the rising sun (and new life) came. There are, however, a few more concrete accounts of posthumous existence. One occurs in the *Book of the Dead*, where the blessed dwell in an agricultural paradise called the Field of Reeds, and another in the *Books of the Netherworld* in which mummies lie inert in the subterranean kingdom of Osiris until, reawakened by the nightly passage of the sun god, they experience a complete human life cycle every twenty four hours. Of these conceptions, the Field of Reeds was perhaps the version of the afterlife which most ancient Egyptians would have desired. It is a kind of idealized version of Egypt, with waterways and cultivated lands, in which the dead are shown plowing, sowing and reaping abundant crops, sailing in boats and enjoying the simple pleasures of life.

Literature:
D'Auria, Lacovara and Roehrig, *Mummies & Magic*, 27-37; Taylor, *Death and the Afterlife*, 10-45.

The ancient Egyptians' notions of the state of existence in which the dead would dwell were many and varied—changing according to the status of the individual and the time at which they lived. But a common theme was that in many ways the hereafter would resemble the environment in which they had lived on earth. This eternal "paradise" was depicted in one of the vignettes of the *Book of the Dead*, that of spell 110.

In the papyrus of Nebseny, draftsman and copyist in the temple of the god Ptah, the vignette shows a schematized landscape known as the Field of Offerings or Field of Reeds. It is a direct successor of the kind of illustration of the hereafter painted on some Middle Kingdom coffins (see Section 3, Mummification, Object EA 30842). In this landscape, various different episodes of the dead man's existence are shown as though taking place simultaneously. Watercourses were dominant features. These waterways bounded agricultural land which produced abundant crops that grew to enormous heights. The dead would be employed in planting and harvesting these crops. Two images on Nebseny's papyrus show him guiding a plow drawn by oxen, while above he is using a sickle to harvest the fully grown crop. These incidents are, of course, all part of the crucial process of nourishing the dead, and appropriately Nebseny also appears seated before a table of offerings. Other features of the scene remind us that this is a divine world. Nebseny is shown adoring gods and burning incense, while a divine barque is represented at lower right.

SCENES OF THE AFTERLIFE
FROM THE BOOK OF THE DEAD
OF NEBSENY

EA 9900/18

Ink on papyrus

Probably from Saqqara

18th Dynasty, c. 1400-1390 bc

Acquired from the collection of James Burton in 1836

Literature: Quirke, *Owners of Funerary Papyri*, 47, 77-8 (No. 124).

THE CREATION OF THE WORLD, FROM THE GREENFIELD PAPYRUS

EA 10554/87

Ink on papyrus

From Deir el-Bahri, the "Royal Cache"

Early 22nd Dynasty, about 940 bc

Height 47.00 cm

Donated by Mrs. Greenfield in 1910

Literature: Budge, *The Greenfield Papyrus in the British Museum*, 79-80, pl. CV-CVII; James, *Egyptian Painting*, 48, fig. 53.

The "Greenfield Papyrus," (which takes its name from a former owner), is one of the longest and most beautifully illustrated manuscripts of the *Book of the Dead* to have survived. Originally, over thirty-seven meters in length, it is now cut into ninety-six separate sheets mounted between glass. It was made for a woman named Nestanebisheru, the daughter of the high priest of Amun Pinedjem II. As a member of the ruling elite at Thebes, she was provided with funerary equipment of very high quality. Many of the spells included on her papyrus are illustrated with small vignettes, and besides these there are several large illustrations depicting important scenes.

One of these scenes, shown here, is a symbolic representation of the creation of the world. According to mythology, this occurred when the sky goddess Nut was raised aloft to form a heavenly canopy above the earth, personified as the god Geb. Here the earth god is shown as a semi-recumbent figure stretching out his limbs while the elongated body of Nut arches above him. Her feet touch the ground at the eastern horizon and her fingers at the western horizon. She is supported by a third key-figure, Shu, god of the atmosphere, who is aided in his task by two ram-headed deities. This scene became a common one on papyri and coffins in the 21st Dynasty, for the process of creation which it depicts was closely linked in the minds of the Egyptians with the renewal of life for the dead. On this papyrus, Nestanebisheru herself kneels at right raising her hands in adoration; her *ba*-spirit imitates her gesture, and a group of gods accompany her.

THE WEIGHING OF THE HEART, FROM THE GREENFIELD PAPYRUS

EA 10554/80

Ink on papyrus

From Deir el-Bahri, the "Royal Cache"

Early 22nd Dynasty, about 940 bc

Height 47.00 cm

Donated by Mrs. Greenfield in 1910

Literature: Budge, *The Greenfield Papyrus in the British Museum*, 73-74, pl. XCIII-XCIV.

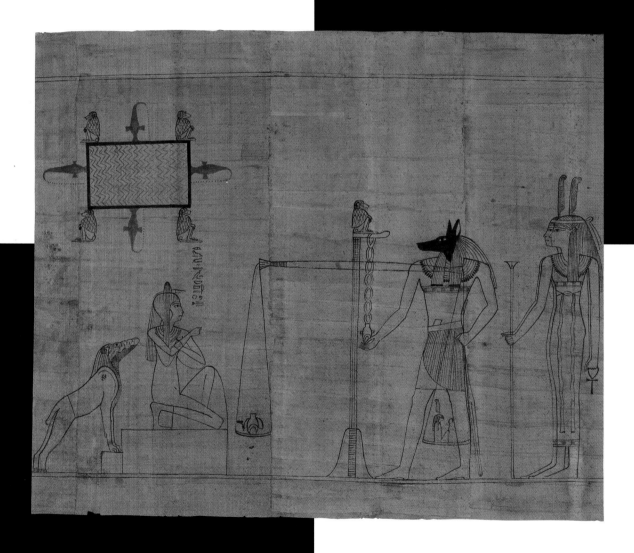

Among the spells of the *Book of the Dead* were many which would enable the deceased to pass safely through obstacles and dangers to reach the afterlife. The tests they faced would establish whether or not the dead person was equipped with the necessary knowledge of the netherworld and its inhabitants. They would also reveal to the gods the nature of that person's conduct while on earth. The most formidable challenge took place in the "Hall of the Two Truths." Here, in the presence of Osiris and forty-two assessor gods, the deceased had first to state that he or she was innocent of a series of specific crimes. But this was not all; to discover the person's true character, the gods would examine the heart.

The ancient Egyptians regarded the heart as the center of an individual's being, and the location of the mind and memory. It was essential that it should not be separated from the body even after death, and for this reason, it was left inside the chest during mummification. When the deceased entered the judgment hall, his or her heart would be tested. This assessment was described and illustrated as a weighing in a balance against an image of *Maat*, the principle of order, right and truth. Only if the heart balanced correctly against *Maat* would the deceased be declared *maa-kheru*. This expression, literally translated "true-of-voice," meant that he or she had lived according to the principles of right and proper conduct and was therefore fit to enter the afterlife.

The description of this symbolic weighing formed one of the most important texts in the *Book of the Dead*, and it was regularly accompanied by a detailed illustration. In this vignette from her papyrus, Nestanebisheru kneels before the balance where her heart is being weighed. The operation is performed by the jackal-headed Anubis, god of embalming and guardian of cemeteries, and sitting atop the scales is a small baboon representing Thoth, the scribe of the gods, who ensured an accurate result. The heart in the left-hand scale pan is shown in perfect balance against *Maat*, which is depicted as a small squatting goddess, whose feather-headdress is the hieroglyphic sign for her name. At the right stands another pair of *Maat*-figures who represent the "Two Truths" for whom the hall is named. At left are two images which indicate what might happen to Nestanebisheru if her heart should reveal that she has lived a life of wickedness. Just behind her stands Ammit ("the devourer"), a monster which is part crocodile, part lion and part hippopotamus. Her task was to swallow the heart, depriving its owner of their very being and condemning them to non-existence. Above is the "Lake of Fire," a place of punishment for the wicked. It is shown in bird's eye view as a pool with stylized ripples, guarded by four baboons; in the middle of each side is the hieroglyphic sign for "fire." For the corpse to be consumed by fire was abhorrent to the Egyptians, as this left no physical "harbor" for the spirit to inhabit, and the result was total annihilation. As in all scenes of the weighing, however, the result for Nestanebisheru is a positive one, for by depicting the deceased as "true of voice" a favorable outcome would be assured.

The papyrus of Ankhwahibre is one of the finest examples of the *Book of the Dead* from the Ptolemaic Period. The penmanship of the vignettes is of exceptional quality. The vignette to spell 125 shows the judgment hall. The roof is supported by columns, and Osiris sits enthroned as judge, under a canopy. Before him are the forty-two assessors in two rows, probably intended to be seated along the walls of the hall. The dead man appears twice, adoring each group, and the accompanying text (not on this section) contains his denial of the crimes which would damn him if he should be found guilty.

The main action of the scene is the weighing of the heart. Anubis and Horus tend the balance, while Thoth with his scribal palette and pen records the outcome. It is favorable to Ankhwahibre for he appears with arms upraised in jubilation, supported by Maat, the goddess who personified the concept of Right and Order. The Devourer Ammit, once again cheated of her prey, sits on a pedestal facing Osiris.

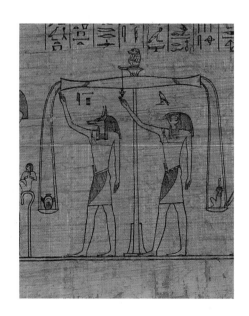

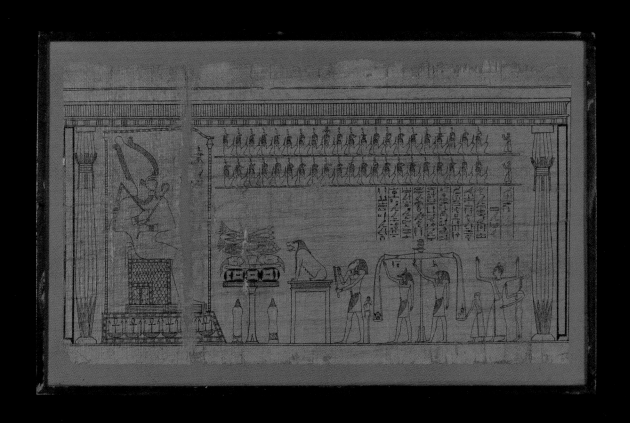

THE JUDGMENT FROM THE PAPYRUS OF ANKHWAHIBRE

EA 10558/18

Ink on papyrus

Provenance unknown

Ptolemaic Period, 305-30 bc

Acquired in 1920

Literature: Quirke, *Owners of Funerary Papyri* 32, 71 (No. 33)

9870

WOODEN MUMMIFORM STATUETTE

EA 9870

Wood coated with resin

Probably from Thebes

22nd Dynasty, about 900 bc

Height 42.3 cm

Acquired in 1843

Papyrus scrolls containing spells from the *Book of the Dead* were often placed inside the coffin of the deceased, and sometimes within the wrappings of the mummy. At the end of the New Kingdom, the texts prepared for private individuals became more varied, and most high-status burials at Thebes were accompanied by two papyri. One of these contained selected spells from the *Book of the Dead*. The other usually bore the title *Amduat*, or "What is in the Netherworld," but its content varied a good deal, comprising elements of one or more of the *Books of the Netherworld* which had been a key feature of the burial equipage of New Kingdom pharaohs. The usual practice in the 21st and 22nd Dynasties was for one roll to be placed within the mummy bandages while the other was secreted within a wooden statuette. This practice is attested as early as the reign of Amenhotep II, whose tomb contained such a figure, but, as often happened, many years elapsed before a custom which had begun as an element of royal ritual spread to the private sphere. Polychrome wooden statuettes made to hold the *Book of the Dead* of private persons are known from the 19th-20th Dynasties; they represented Osiris wearing his characteristic *atef* crown and holding royal scepters. Later, statuettes such as this one were painted black or coated with a dark resin. Although more austere in appearance they undoubtedly continued to represent Osiris, since some of them wear his distinctive headgear. In some instances the figure itself was hollow, the papyrus fitting into a slot cut into the back and closed with a wooden lid. Otherwise, as here, the cavity was carved into the base. Originally, the papyrus roll would have been concealed by a wooden cover fitted into the slot.

41552

Osiris, supreme god of resurrection, was closely associated with the life-giving forces of nature, particularly the Nile and vegetation. Above all, he was connected with germinating grain. The emergence of a living, growing, plant from the apparently dormant seed hidden within the earth was regarded by the Egyptians as a metaphor for the rebirth of a human being from the lifeless husk of the corpse. The concept was translated into physical form by the fashioning of images of Osiris out of earth and grain. These "corn-mummies" were composed of sand or mud, mixed with grains of barley. They generally have Osirian attributes and are often represented with an erect penis, symbolizing fecundity. As in this instance, the "mummy" is sometimes wrapped in linen bandages and may possess a finely detailed mask of wax, representing the face of Osiris.

A few small figures of this type have been found within the wrappings of mummies, but in general they were not destined for the tomb. The majority were made according to an elaborate ritual which took place during the annual festival of Osiris in the month of Khoiak, the fourth month of the inundation season. This was intended to ensure the god's resurrection and, by extension, the continuation of life in Egypt and the maintenance of the ordered universe. The corn-mummies were then carefully buried in sacred spots specially designated for this purpose. In the most typical examples the mummy was placed inside a miniature anthropoid coffin of painted wood, which had the head of a falcon, probably alluding to the god Sokar, who usually took this form.

CORN MUMMY IN WOODEN COFFIN

EA 41552

Mummy: earth, linen wrappings, wax

Coffin: painted wood

Provenance unrecorded

Late Period, 664-305 bc

Height 58.4 cm

Acquired in 1905

Literature: for these figures in general: Raven, *Oudheidkundige Mededelingen uit het Rijksmuseum van Oudheden te Leiden*, 63 (1982), 7-38.

STATUETTE OF PTAH-SOKAR-OSIRIS

EA 47577

Painted wood

From Asyut (excavated by D.G. Hogarth 1906-1907)

Late Period, 664-305 bc

Height 53.5 cm; Length 28.5 cm

An important element of high-status burials in the Late Period and Ptolemaic Period was a wooden statuette of a mummiform deity who is identified as Ptah-Sokar-Osiris. This entity is an example of syncretism, that merging of the characteristics of one or more deities so characteristic of ancient Egyptian religious expression. In this instance, each of the component gods was a powerful figure in his own right, Ptah and Osiris in particular being associated with the powers of creation, while Sokar was an ancient god of the Memphite necropolis. The merging of Osiris and Sokar had begun as early as the Middle Kingdom, and with the addition of Ptah the resulting tripartite god became especially prominent as a guarantor of resurrection after death.

A statuette such as this was provided in most elite tombs of the Late Period. The external appearance of the god is derived chiefly from that of Osiris. The body is enveloped in a shroud, which is often colored red. The headdress is the *atef* crown, composed of ram's horns, a sun-disc and twin feathers. This statuette is uninscribed, but on others a hieroglyphic text refers to the deceased owner sharing in the renewal of life enjoyed by Osiris. The bases of these statuettes are also important. They are often highly decorated with architectural facade designs, suggesting identification with the tomb, and there is often a cavity in the base. This cavity can be covered by a wooden falcon (as here) or even a complete model of a coffin. A miniature corn mummy has been found in some examples, although in this instance the hollow space beneath the falcon is empty.

FIGURE OF THE BA

EA 61884

Painted wood

Provenance unknown

Ptolemaic Period, 305-30 bc

Height 10.2 cm; Width 4.0 cm

Acquired in 1835

Literature: *Art and Afterlife in Ancient Egypt*, No. 62.

The *ba* was one of a person's non-physical aspects, or modes of existence. It symbolized the individual's ability to move freely, and was supposed to leave the tomb and fly to join the sun god in the sky. On account of this role, the *ba* was regularly depicted in the form of a bird with a human head (and often also with human arms). However, in order to ensure eternal life, the *ba* had to return to the burial chamber periodically to be reunited with the mummy.

In this small figurine, the *ba* wears a beard, a wig and a collar—appropriate elements of the appearance of the blessed dead. Though carved in rudimentary fashion and simply painted in red, blue and black, it coveys a sense of vigor and has a naive charm. A wooden peg projecting from the base indicates that it was once fixed to some larger object. Small wooden figures of the *ba* such as this were sometimes placed on coffins or mounted on the top of wooden funerary stelae.

3

Mummification

The artificial preservation of the dead body was one of the hallmarks of ancient Egyptian civilization, provoking the curiosity of other peoples in ancient times just as much as it does today. Mummification was practiced in Egypt for 4000 years, and its history was complex. In the pharaonic period the practice was explained in terms of religious beliefs current at that time: thus the corpse had to be preserved to act as a base for the *ba*-spirit, and undergoing the mummification process identified the dead person closely with Osiris. Recent discoveries have shown, however, that mummification in Egypt began earlier than was previously thought and that its origins were complex. As early as 3500 *bc*, bodies buried in the cemeteries of Hierakonpolis were treated with resin, wrapped in linen and even eviscerated—all features associated with the "classic" embalming procedures of later periods. Also in this early period the corpse was sometimes dismembered and the bones reassembled before wrapping. Interpretations of this custom vary, but among the motivating factors may have been the removal of the perishable soft tissues which produced foul-smelling corruption fluids, and the incapacitating of the dead to prevent them from returning to trouble the living.

In the historic period, dismemberment was abandoned, and a formal process of treatment for the corpse was gradually evolved. The purpose of this was not so much to preserve the corpse exactly as it had appeared in life, but to transform the perishable and imperfect earthly body into an eternal image, perfect and endowed with divine attributes. The Egyptians left few writings describing how this was done, but the process can be reconstructed from accounts by Classical authors such as Herodotus and Diodorus Siculus, together with examinations of the mummies themselves and laboratory experiments aimed at replicating the techniques. Using these sources, embalming at its best can be reconstructed as follows.

Immediately after death the corpse was washed and eviscerated to remove the most perishable organs before decomposition set in. The embalmers performed these tasks with minimal intervention: the brain was usually extracted via the nose, and the organs of the chest cavity through a small incision in the left side of the abdomen. The heart, regarded as the center of the intelligence, was left in place (the brain was disposed of), while liver, lungs, stomach and intestines (sometimes also the kidneys) were set aside for separate preservation.

Having removed the most corruptible parts, the embalmers purged the body of its fluids. To do this they used a naturally-occurring compound of alkaline salts known as natron. Linen bags filled with this substance were tightly packed inside the body cavity, and more natron was heaped over the corpse. After thirty-five to forty days the salt had absorbed all the liquid content of the body, leaving it completely desiccated. In this sterile environment the bacteria which cause decomposition could not flourish.

Removed from the natron, the body would have appeared very shriveled. The natron broke down the subcutaneous fats, leaving the skin leathery and slack. The embalmers now set about replacing the corrupt parts with various materials which had both practical and symbolic functions. The cavities were filled with sawdust, spices, dried plants, earth and bundles of linen. In addition, molten resin was often poured into the skull and chest, and the skin was anointed with the same material. This would help to give the body a pleasant smell, and also symbolically conferred divine status on the deceased. In the Third Intermediate Period, the embalmers took exceptional trouble to beautify the body, using methods familiar to modern taxidermists; thus sand, mud, and linen were inserted beneath the skin to restore fullness of form, the hair was elaborately arranged, and artificial eyes of stone or colored glass were inserted under the eyelids, giving the impression that the deceased was alive and awake.

No doubt all of these operations were accompanied by the recitation of prayers and the performance of rituals. This applied particularly to the final stages of mummification, the wrapping of the body. Wrapping in linen is attested as early as the mid-4th millennium *bc*. At that time it probably served the practical function of keeping all the body parts together, but in the historic period it became a key means of promoting the elevation of the dead to divine status. The *Ritual of Embalming*, one of the few documentary sources that describe the procedure, reveals that the individual cloths were associated with gods and goddesses. The external appearance of the mummy was of the greatest importance, for it proclaimed that the deceased had become a transfigured being. In the Old Kingdom the body was made up to resemble a statue, the arms, legs, fingers and toes separately wrapped and the head and face modeled in plaster or resin-soaked linen, and it was dressed in clothes. About the 21st century *bc* this method of presentation was superseded by the more familiar image of a shrouded person, the limbs confined within tight wrappings. Often only the head was modeled and this was usually represented by an idealized mask. This form, called the *sah*, was derived in part from early depictions of gods. It therefore signified the newly-acquired divinity of the deceased, and the cocoon of wrappings was also a kind of symbolic chrysalis containing the potential for new life.

Relatively little is known about the men who carried out mummification. In the Old Kingdom, when mummification was reserved for the elite of society, they seem to have been few in number. The knowledge required to mummify a corpse was a closely guarded secret, accessible only to a privileged few. But with the passage of time mummification became more widely available. Herodotus mentions that in his time (c. 450 *bc*) there were three distinct methods of treating the corpse, varying according to cost, and this is borne out by examinations of mummies of the later centuries. Contracts on papyrus and ostraca (flakes of limestone or potsherds used for writing notes) survive from the Ptolemaic and Roman Periods, in which clients agree upon a price with the embalmers for the mummification of a relative's body. The duration of the process varied, but seventy days is most commonly mentioned as the time required for embalming a body and preparing it for burial.

The final act in the process took place at the entrance to the tomb on the day of burial. Here the mummy underwent a crucial ritual, the "Opening of the Mouth." Religious texts were recited, offerings were made, and priests touched the eyes, nose, ears and mouth of the mummy-mask with a range of tools and instruments, symbolically "opening" each aperture and restoring to the dead person the use of his bodily faculties.

In all but the very poorest burials, the mummy was placed in a coffin. Persons of wealth and high rank might have two, three or even four coffins, one inside the other. These held magical significance far beyond their basic function of physically protecting the body. The coffin could function symbolically as an eternal dwelling, as a sacred environment in which the deceased could exist, even as a small-scale re-creation of the universe with the dead person cast in the role of creator-god. These associations were manifested in the shape of the coffins and through the images and inscriptions placed on their surfaces, aspects which underwent constant evolution. Indeed, the rich iconography of the coffins tells us more about the Egyptians' notions of the afterlife than could ever be learned from the mummies themselves.

Literature:
Taylor, *Death and Afterlife*; Ikram and Dodson, *The Mummy in Ancient Egypt*.

COFFIN OF NEKHTANKH

EA 35285

Painted wood

From Deir el-Bersha

12th Dynasty

Height 62.0 cm; Width 60.2 cm; Length 213.2 cm

Acquired in 1901

Literature: Porter and Moss, IV, 187; Seipel, *Ägypten*, 96 (No. 62); Willems, *Chests of Life*, 35 (B6); Lapp, *Typologie*, 276 (B10); Davies in Davies and Schofield, *Egypt, the Aegean and the Levant*, 147.

The standard form for coffins in the Old and Middle Kingdoms was the rectangular chest with a flat or vaulted lid. The material of which the coffin was made influenced its cost and reflected the status of the owner. Cheaper coffins were made of woods native to Egypt, such as sycamore fig. For persons of higher rank coffins were carved from stone or assembled from planks of costly imported timbers such as cedar. In this instance, the owner Nekhtankh is not given any title in the inscriptions, but he was evidently a person of importance, as his coffin is made of cedar and has been decorated by skilled craftsmen. The inscriptions, in particular, are the work of a careful scribe and illustrate the highest quality of hieroglyphic palaeography in the Middle Kingdom.

Although the images and texts are quite sparse they reflect some of the important symbolic functions of the coffin. The most fundamental of these was the provision of new life and sustenance for the deceased. A pair of eyes is painted within a frame towards the end of one of the long sides. When the mummified body was placed inside the coffin it was carefully positioned on its left side, with the head supported by a head-rest. The mummy's face was aligned with the eyes painted on the side of the coffin, and these operated magically to enable the dead person to see. By orientating the coffin in the tomb so that the side with the eyes faced east, the deceased could view the rising sun each dawn, symbolic of new life, and could also look towards the part of his tomb where offerings would be placed to sustain his spirit. The long inscriptions on the sides of the coffin refer to this same basic necessity, for they contain the *hetep-di-nesu* formula, in which Osiris is invoked to supply offerings. Other elements of coffin decoration alluded to the rituals which were carried out at the funeral. Some of these rites were re-enactments of mythical events, in which priests took the roles of the gods and goddesses involved, and these deities are named on the sides of Nekhtankh's coffin. Isis and Nephthys, the sisters of Osiris, are mentioned at the foot and head-ends, respectively, and on the long sides the texts place Nekhtankh under the protection of Geb, Nut, Shu, Tefnut and the Four Sons of Horus. No supreme creator-god is named in these texts, and this was because the deceased himself, inside the coffin, was cast in the most important role of all, that of Osiris or Re (and sometimes as both gods simultaneously). The inscriptional program, then, sets the stage for an unending replay of these crucial rites—all of which were directed towards the chief goal, that of bringing new life to the dead.

Egyptian coffins possessed highly complex symbolism. Through their physical form and the images and inscriptions on their surfaces they were believed to create a sacred environment in which the rebirth of the occupant could take place. Thus, in a rectangular coffin of the Middle Kingdom, the internal space demarcated by the walls was potentially more important than the exterior because these surfaces were immediately accessible to the dead person. This explains why the interior decoration of these coffins is much more detailed and elaborate than the exterior.

This phenomenon is well exemplified by the finely painted inner coffin made for Seni, an official of the governor of the Hare province, who was buried at Deir el-Bersha. The exterior is carefully painted, with an eye-panel and standard texts, much the same as on the coffin of Nekhtankh, though here the texts are not evocations of funerary ritual but references to the protection given to the dead man by the goddess Nut. But it is inside the coffin that the richest decoration is to be seen. A "false door" and a table of offerings are painted close to the head of the deceased, enabling his spirit to pass freely in and out of the coffin and to receive nourishment. Elsewhere the walls are divided horizontally into zones. At the top is an elongated hieroglyph for "sky," a blue vault studded with stars; below this comes a large inscription promising that Seni will receive offerings and enjoy a state of blessedness. Next comes the "frieze of objects," a narrow band filled with pictures of granaries, items of clothing, pieces of jewelry, tools, weapons, furniture, vessels and many other commodities which the wealthy Egyptian desired for his afterlife. Their names are written above them. Among these objects there are also amulets and items of royal regalia, such as scepters and kingly headdresses; these would magically assimilate the dead man, whatever his rank in life, to Osiris, ruler of the netherworld.

It was of course supposed that these objects would become real when Seni required them in the next life. But he would also need sacred knowledge, information about the perilous journey he had to make to the netherworld, so that he might reach it safely. To equip him, large areas of the coffin sides were inscribed in ink with religious writings now known as the *Coffin Texts*. These compositions derived ultimately from the *Pyramid Texts*, inscribed in the burial chambers of kings of the 5th and 6th Dynasties. These spells offer much magical assistance to the deceased, including a diagram of the realm that he would reach, complete with waterways, canals, islands and settlements, all neatly labeled. On the floor of the coffin is a composition called the *Book of Two Ways*, another guide to the hereafter in which again paths and watercourses are marked out for the deceased's guidance. The location of this text on the base is another reflection of the notion that the images inside the coffin created a fully three-dimensional "world" in which the deceased could travel and dwell.

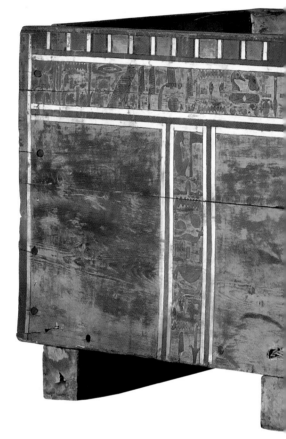

INNER COFFIN OF SENI

EA 30842

Painted wood

From Deir el-Bersha

12th Dynasty, about 1850 bc

Height 73 cm; Width 62 cm; Length 215 cm

Acquired in 1899

Literature: Spencer, *Death in Ancient Egypt*, 171-2, pl. 24.

ENDS OF THE COFFIN OF INTEF

EA 46644

Painted cedarwood

Asyut (tomb 46; excavated by David G. Hogarth in 1906-1907)

12th Dynasty

Foot: Height 57.7 cm; Width 57.5 cm; Thickness 6.2 cm

Literature: Seipel, *Ägypten*, 95 (No. 61a, b); Davies in Davies and Schofield, 146.

These boards formed the head and foot-ends of a rectangular wooden coffin. It is made of cedarwood and the along the edges are stripes of bright yellow paint, which substitute for the gold leaf that would have been found on the finest coffins. Nonetheless, this specimen—of which only these two pieces survive—was of high quality and was extensively decorated. The exterior of each end is adorned with an inscription in three horizontal and three vertical lines. These texts contain abbreviated versions of spells 31 and 32 of the *Coffin Texts*. Spell 32, located at the foot-end of the coffin, is an address to the god Osiris: "Hail to you! He eases your pain, O Osiris in Djedu. This Intef has come to the place where you are. He will drive away your pain; he will make your foes tremble..." Here the deceased Intef is cast in the role of the god Horus, who defends and supports his father.[1] Spell 31, at the head-end, promises the deceased that he shall see the falcons on their nests and the birth of the sacred bull Apis; he is equated with these youthful deities, and is also assured that he will see Osiris in Djedu. Besides these texts, carefully carved into the wood and filled with blue pigment, are the names of the Four Sons of Horus, marking their stations at each corner of the coffin to protect the deceased and to take part in the eternal repetition of funerary rituals.

On the interior are painted texts and images which formed part of the "frieze of objects." At the head a large inscription declares the deceased "revered before Osiris," and below is a list of oils and images of commodities: jars of oils, a headrest, a mirror in its case and a harp. The foot-end declares Intef "revered before the Great God, lord of Heaven" and shows a granary, complete with domed grain bins and columns with lotus capitals. This would symbolically provide the deceased with an endless supply of food. Below the granary, appropriately located at the foot of the coffin, are sandals.

On the roughly chamfered surfaces of the joints are short incised inscriptions which would have been hidden once the coffin was assembled. These texts allude to the rites supposed to be carried out in the embalming place on the night before the burial. Important gods and goddesses of the Osirian myth-cycle are invoked, to strengthen the body of the deceased, to protect him and to ensure his rebirth. These texts, hidden within the fabric of Middle Kingdom coffins, were later written prominently on the exterior surfaces of coffins in the New Kingdom, and were accompanied by images of the deities referred to.[2]

[1] The translation given here is an emendation, since the pronouns in the original are confused

2 Grallert, *Studien zur Altägyptischen Kultur* 23 (1996), 147-165

LID OF A RISHI COFFIN

EA 52951

Sycamore fig wood, painted

From Birabi, Thebes (intrusive burial in tomb 46/47; excavated

by Howard Carter and Lord Carnarvon)

Late 17th or early 18th Dynasty, about 1600-1500 bc

Height (including case) 59.5 cm; Width 46 cm; Length 191 cm

Acquired in 1914

Literature: Davies in Davies and Schofield, *Egypt, the Aegean and the Levant*, 148, pl. 32, 3. On *rishi* coffins in general, see Ikram and Dodson, *The Mummy in Ancient Egypt*, 204-6; Taylor, *Death and the Afterlife*, 223-4.

Anthropoid or mummiform coffins were introduced into Egyptian burials during the Middle Kingdom, around 2000-1800 *bc*. Their appearance reflected that of the mummy itself very closely and, as the outer shell of the body, they should be distinguished in function from the rectangular coffins within which they were usually enclosed. In the Second Intermediate Period another anthropoid type was developed, probably at Thebes. At this time the Asiatic Hyksos rulers, based in the Nile Delta, enjoyed supreme power in Egypt. The Upper Egyptian kings no longer had unrestricted access to the luxury products of the eastern Mediterranean, and in consequence fine-grained imported wood was in short supply. Most coffins at Thebes were now crudely made from local timber, and had narrow, wedge-shaped faces. These anthropoid cases were produced as an alternative to the rectangular coffins rather than as part of a set. Their most characteristic feature was the decoration of the lid with a pattern of feathers; their modern name, *Rishi* coffins, derives from an Arabic word meaning "feather" and was bestowed on them by 19th century archaeologists.

The precise interpretation of the feathered design remains a matter for debate. Among the most favored theories are that the deceased is depicted under the protective wings of goddesses, or that the entire lid is a representation of the dead person as a *ba*. In most instances, the feathered patterning does not extend to the case of the coffin, which was usually painted a uniform blue or occasionally bore figured scenes.

This *rishi* coffin was discovered by Howard Carter and Lord Carnarvon during the excavation of a large Middle Kingdom tomb in an area of the Theban necropolis known as the Birabi. The tomb had been reused in the 17th or early 18th Dynasty and was found to contain many burials of private individuals. The coffin is partly hollowed out from the trunk of a sycamore fig tree, and partly constructed from pieces of wood rather roughly joined together. The headdress, as well as the body, is covered with stylized feathers. On the breast is a vulture with outspread wings and beneath this a standard offering formula written in clumsily formed hieroglyphs. The frontal surface of the feet is decorated with two confronted figures of the god Anubis.

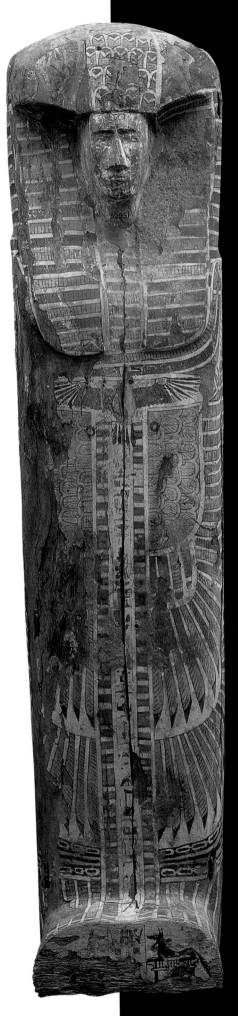

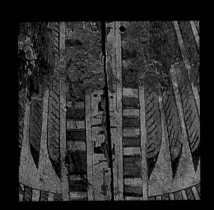

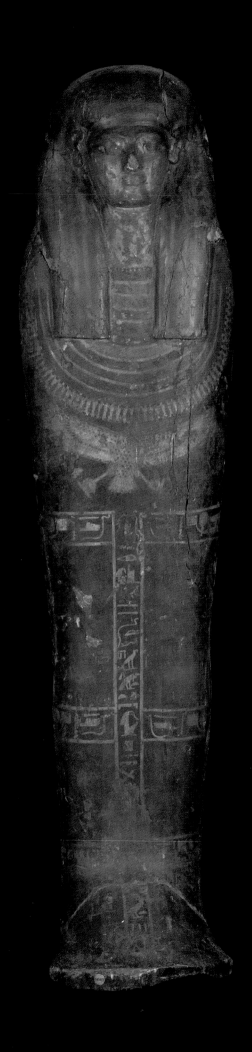

COFFIN OF TAMYT

EA 6661

Wood, gessoed, painted and varnished

Probably from Thebes

18th Dynasty, about 1400 bc

Height 64 cm; Width 50 cm; Length 198 cm

Date of acquisition unknown

Literature: Serpico in Nicholson and Shaw, *Ancient Egyptian Materials and Technology*, 460, 461, fig. 18.21.

During the New Kingdom, there was a decline in the popularity of rectangular coffins. In their place, the anthropoid or mummiform type became the predominant form. The *rishi* design continued to be used on royal coffins, but those of private individuals were decorated in a new style. This specimen, inscribed for a woman named Tamyt, illustrates many of the typical features of this new pattern. On the breast, below the collar, is painted a vulture with outspread wings. This represents the sky-goddess Nut, and in a vertical inscription in the center of the lid she is summoned to spread herself in protection over the dead person. Further divine aid is given by the god Anubis and the Four Sons of Horus. They are named in the lateral bands of inscription which begin in the center of the lid and continue down the sides of the coffin-case.

Inscribing the names of gods along the sides of the coffin was a practice which had originated in the Middle Kingdom. Besides alluding to important funerary rituals, these texts provided a kind of protective encirclement for the mummy inside. During the 18th Dynasty it became customary to paint images of the gods close to their texts to give additional protection, as here on the coffin of Tamyt.

The use of a black background for this coffin reflects the symbolic connotations which that color possessed in Egyptian religious attitudes. Black was the color of the fertile, life-giving mud of Egypt, and was therefore associated with resurrection. Gods who held the power to renew life were sometimes depicted with black skin or black-colored bodies, so by coloring the outer envelope of the mummy in a similar way, an identification between deceased and deity was invoked. Scientific analysis has established that the black varnish on this coffin was derived from bitumen, making it one of the earliest attested uses of this substance in ancient Egyptian funerary practices.[1]

Nothing definite is known about Tamyt, but her family was probably not among the wealthiest at Thebes, since this coffin was not made specifically for her. A standard selection of texts was inscribed, with blank spaces left, into which the name of the eventual owner could be inserted. This is clear on the case of the coffin, where Tamyt's name was written in paint of a slightly lighter color than that of the surrounding texts, and was squeezed into the rather inadequate spaces left by the first scribe.

[1] Serpico, 460.

The chief purpose of ancient Egyptian funerary rituals (including mummification) was to enable the individual to pass from the earthly life to a new existence, in which he or she would possess the attributes of divine beings. The outward appearance of the transfigured dead would reflect their new, god-like status. For this reason all images of the dead, whether mummy-masks, anthropoid coffins or free-standing statues, were idealized, representing the individual as eternally youthful and free from all physical disabilities or blemishes.

This face once formed part of the lid of a mummiform coffin. The large tenon at the top slotted into the wig, and a single wooden dowel through this held the face in position; a bituminous adhesive was also applied. Although the face presents a generic image of the resurrected dead person, it is, nonetheless, a superb example of wood-carving. The facial contours, in particular the cheeks, nose and mouth, have been rendered with great sensitivity. The inlaid eyes give a wonderfully vivid and alert impression, a perfect expression of the ancient Egyptians' conviction that the dead would reawaken to a new existence.

FACE OF A COFFIN

EA 6887

Wood, eyes of obsidian and ivory set in bronze sockets

Provenance unknown

18th Dynasty, c. 1400 bc or later

Height 23 cm; Width 14 cm

Acquired from the collection of Joseph Sams in 1834

Literature: Quirke, *Ancient Egyptian Religion*, 146-7, fig. 86.

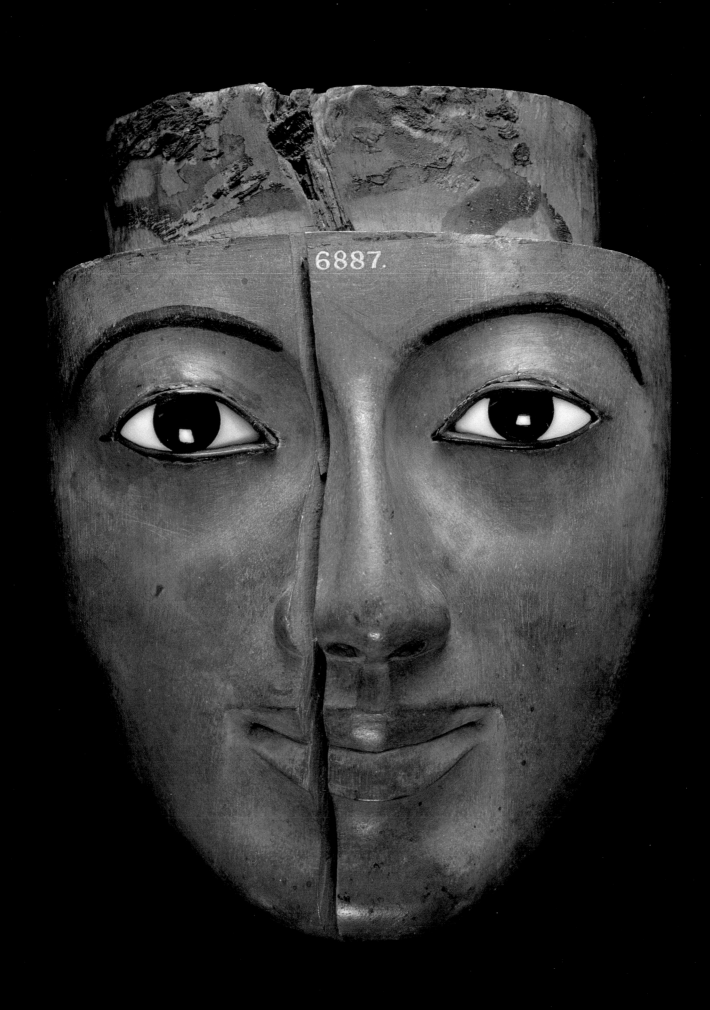

6887.

The hieroglyphic inscription on this mummy-case states that Tjayasetimu was a "Singer of the Interior of Amun." Many women of high rank at Thebes held this title during the 22nd Dynasty. They were subordinates of the God's Wife (or Divine Adoratrice) of Amun, the supreme priestess of the god, who was usually a member of the royal family. The "singers" were mainly selected from the high-ranking families of Thebes, and their main duty was to provide musical accompaniment to the temple rituals, primarily by singing or chanting, but perhaps also by playing instruments. Like the God's Wife herself, the singers were obliged to remain celibate.[1] X-rays of the mummy in this case show that Tjayasetimu died around the age of 12. Her skeleton is in good condition and shows no signs of injury. Packing, probably a mixture of sand and sawdust, can be seen filling the abdominal cavity; it is thought that packages containing the embalmed viscera may be embedded within this material.

The linen-wrapped body is enclosed within a cartonnage case, a mummy-shaped shell made from layers of linen, glue and plaster. This one seems to have been designed to accommodate a larger person, as the mummy's head only reaches as far as the shoulders of the case. The case itself has been carefully modeled to represent the deceased as though she were alive, with the left arm held across the breast, the right (carved from a separate piece of wood) at the side, and the feet uncovered. This pose occurs mainly on coffins of the 19th and 20th Dynasties, but it was occasionally revived at later periods. On other examples the individual is usually shown dressed in the clothes of the living, but here the surface of the body is covered with painted figures of deities. Before Tjayasetimu was placed in her tomb, the surface of her cartonnage case was covered almost entirely with a black resinous substance which obscures the decoration (selective cleaning has been carried out in modern times to reveal the gilded face and the inscription). This blackening can be seen on other mummy-cases of the same period, sometimes carefully applied over the whole surface with a brush, and in other cases apparently poured on to the body just before it was placed in the tomb. Although the precise significance of this ritual act is unknown, both resin and the color black had powerful magical associations for the ancient Egyptians. Coating the mummy with this substance may have conferred divine status and new life on the deceased.[2]

[1] for the role of these women, see Naguib, *Le clergé féminin d'Amon thébain à la 21e Dynastie*, 206-7, 224, 232-5.

[2] for coffins and cartonnages coated with black libations: Niwinski; Taylor in D'Auria, Lacovara and Roehrig, *Mummies and Magic*, 220-1.

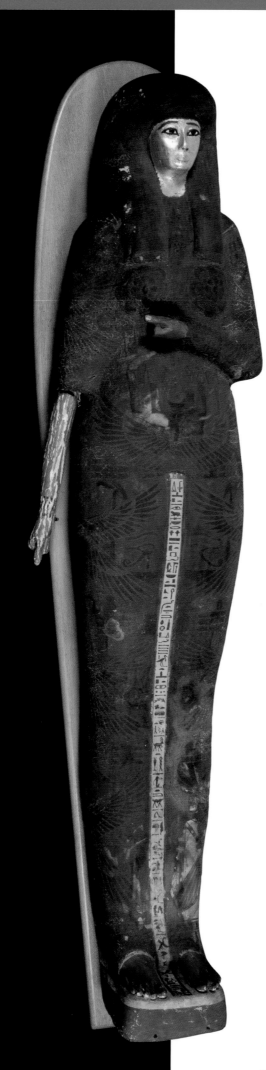

MUMMY OF TJAYASETIMU IN CARTONNAGE CASE

EA 20744

Cartonnage and wood, painted and gilded

From Thebes

22nd Dynasty, about 900 bc

Length 1.51 cm

Acquired in 1888

Literature: Dawson and Gray, *Mummies*, 19-20, frontispiece b, pl. Xa (No. 35); Andrews, *Egyptian Mummies*, 2nd ed. 55, fig. 50; Niwinski, *Studia Aegyptiaca* 14 463-4; *Art and Afterlife in Ancient Egypt*, No. 112.

MUMMY OF PADIAMENET IN PAINTED CARTONNAGE CASE

EA 6682

Probably from Thebes

25th Dynasty, about 700 bc

Length 1.76 cm

Acquired from the collection of Anastasi in 1839

Literature: Dawson and Gray, *Mummies*, 14-15, pl. VIId
(No. 26); *Art and Afterlife in Ancient Egypt*, No. 113.

Padiamenet, who apparently died in his thirties according to x-rays of his mummy, was an attendant and doorkeeper of the god Re at Thebes, as was his father Usermose. He seems to have been buried in a tomb somewhere on the Theban West Bank, probably with other members of his family. A set of coffins inscribed for a Usermose, son of Padiamenet, now in Brussels, probably belonged to a son of the British Museum's Padiamenet, since this Usermose was also an official of the cult of Re and the coffins of both men were formerly in the collection of the Swedish-Norwegian consul Giovanni Anastasi.

Padiamenet's mummy was interred in a wooden coffin of rather plain design, and an inner case of cartonnage—a lightweight fabric made from layers of linen, glued together and plastered. Such cases were often constructed by pasting the layers of cloth over a core of mud and straw, which was afterwards discarded. The fully-wrapped mummy was then placed inside the hollow cartonnage shell which was laced up at the back like a shoe. This procedure would have required careful wrapping of the mummy to ensure that it fitted comfortably into the case, and in this instance the embalmers seem to have experienced difficulties. X-rays show that the top of the skull only reaches as far as the shoulders of the case. In consequence, the feet projected at the end and to conceal this, the cartonnage was extended by the addition of further cloth.

The surface decoration is arranged in horizontal registers. The first scene, on the chest, shows Padiamenet adoring Osiris and Isis, with the Four Sons of Horus standing in pairs at the sides. Below is a falcon, identified as Osiris-Sokar, and beneath this the domed and feathered fetish of Abydos. This emblem was another representation of Osiris, and it is shown under the protection of the goddesses Neith and Selkis and two ram-headed deities, one of whom is named as Khnum. Jackals on the feet represent the god Wepwawet, the "Opener of the ways"—one of whose roles was to guide the dead in safety to the hereafter. All these images are painted in polychrome and varnished, and are balanced by inscriptions in large blue hieroglyphs on a white ground which stand out all the more clearly on account of the intentional absence of varnish. Along each side is another long inscription invoking Osiris to provide funerary offerings for the dead man.

TWO COFFINS OF NESTAWEDJAT

EA 22812

EA 22813

Probably from Thebes[1]

25th Dynasty, about 700-680 bc

Inner coffin: Height 177.00 cm; Width 56.00 cm

Acquired in 1880

Literature: *Art and Afterlife in Ancient Egypt*, No. 27.

Nestawedjat, the owner of these splendid coffins, was the daughter of a man named Djedmutefankh and a woman named Djedasetesankh. They were probably members of one of the influential families who held high office in the Theban temple hierarchies during the period of Kushite rule over Egypt (25th Dynasty), but their precise place in this society has yet to be determined. The inscriptions on the coffins also describe Nestawedjat as "revered before her husband." This formula, common on funerary monuments of the Old Kingdom, is used here as a conscious piece of archaism; the revival of literary and artistic forms from the days of Egypt's past was a major characteristic of the 25th Dynasty. The words may also indicate that it was the unnamed husband who had commissioned Nestawedjat's burial outfit. The mummy which is associated with these coffins adds nothing to what the inscriptions tell us, for x-rays have shown that it is the body of a man and it has been dated to the 21st Dynasty (about 1000 bc).[2] It may have been substituted for the remains of Nestawedjat by a 19th century antiquities dealer.

The original burial ensemble of Nestawedjat comprised three anthropoid wooden coffins, of which these are the second and third.[3] However, its shape and decoration resembles the outer coffin of Shepenmehyt (see this section, object EA 22814). The larger of the two coffins displayed here has a striking face, enlivened by the use of inlaid eyes set into bronze sockets. The surface of the body is simply decorated with a line of inscription on the lid and another around the case, both texts addressing the gods to provide funerary offerings. Within the case of the coffin is painted a figure of the Goddess of the West, a manifestation of Hathor, who protected the dead in their tombs.

The inner coffin, again with inlaid eyes, is more richly decorated. It was common for the innermost casing, which was in closest proximity to the corpse, to receive the most elaborate paintings. Here the entire surface, both inside and out, has been gessoed and covered with religious images and texts. The maternal sky-goddess Nut spreads her wings over the breast, and the lower compartments of the lid are occupied by deities who offer protection in speeches which are inscribed alongside their figures: the Four Sons of Horus, Horus himself, the earth-god Geb, and two forms of Anubis. Two large *wedjat* eyes and a figure of Isis complete the designs of the lid, while the back is entirely covered with inscriptions. These are rather long-winded and repetitive versions of the *hetep-di-nesu* offering formula. Inside are further images and texts, brightly painted on white and yellow backgrounds. The vertical orientation of the decoration expresses the confident hope that the resurrected deceased will stand up under the life-giving rays of the sun—hence the painting of the solar disc in the space above the mummy's head. Directly before the mummy's face is a scene showing the heart on a standard, protected by two deities. Spells 27 and 28 of the *Book of the Dead* have vignettes similar to this one and both are concerned with ensuring that the heart of the deceased (the center of her being) should not be taken away after death. The corresponding area behind the head shows another two deities, unidentified, and before and behind the feet are images of Isis and Nephthys, their hands raised in a gesture of lamentation. As these goddesses mourned for the murdered Osiris and were instrumental in restoring him to life, the presence of their figures on this coffin was believed to ensure resurrection also for Nestawedjat.

[1] Porter and Moss V, 24, list this set as from Akhmim, but this appears to be an error. The *hetep-di-nesu* formula on the lid of EA 22812 specifies that the deceased should be buried at Thebes, and the style of the coffins is typical of Theban workmanship.

[2] British Museum EA 22812B.

[3] The outermost coffin, EA 22813, is in a poorer state of preservation than its companions.

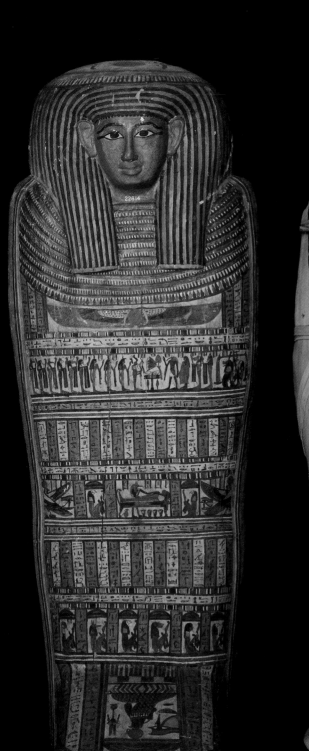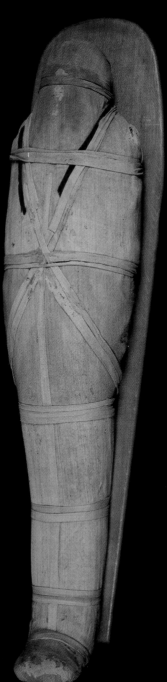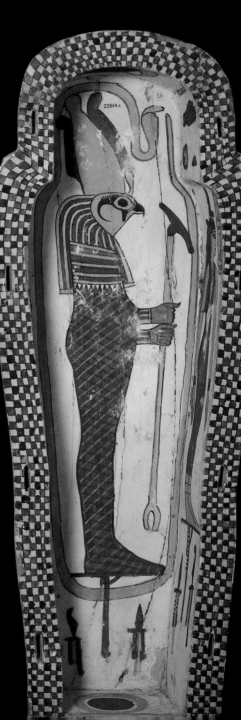

TWO COFFINS AND MUMMY OF SHEPENMEHYT

EA 22814

Painted wood

From Thebes

26th Dynasty, about 600 bc

Outer coffin: Height 2.03 cm

Inner coffin: Height 1.71 cm

Mummy: Length 1.67 cm

Presented by the Prince of Wales (later King Edward VII) in 1869

Literature: Porter and Moss, I, ii, 673; Dawson and Gray, *Mummies*, 15, pl. VIIIa, XXVIIIa (No. 27); Andrews, *Egyptian Mummies*, 2nd ed. 63, figs. 63-64; Taylor in Davies, *Colour and Painting*, pl. 54 (3); Taylor in Strudwick and Taylor, *Theban Necropolis*, pl. 75.

Shepenmehyt was provided with a set of two anthropoid coffins, fitting one inside the other. Both are strikingly decorated with a profusion of texts and images in bright colors. The outermost lid displays a standard sequence of images which recall key elements of funerary mythology. On the breast is the winged solar disc, and below, a narrow scene showing the weighing of the deceased's heart (at right). This is the all-important moment of judgment, which was supposed to determine whether or not the individual was worthy to enter the afterlife. As usual, a successful outcome is shown, and the "justified" Shepenmehyt is introduced to a long line of deities. Further down is a small image of Anubis tending the mummy of Shepenmehyt as it lies on a bier, while figures of other deities give symbolic protection; short columns of text are interspersed among these images, and a large inscription is painted around the sides of the case. On the interior of the case is a large mummiform figure grasping the *was* scepter (symbolizing dominion) and wearing the feathered *atef* crown, a distinctive attribute of Osiris. His head, however, is that of a falcon and from inscribed images of the same type on other coffins it is clear that this is the composite resurrection-deity Ptah-Sokar-Osiris. The mummy lying inside the coffin would be closely identified with this god to ensure rebirth into the afterlife. Isis and Nephthys are depicted at each side to lend their protection, and the sun-disc above the head casts life-renewing rays. The checkered pattern on the thickness of the case is a feature found on other outer coffins made at Thebes at the same period, and may be distinctive of a particular workshop or team of craftsmen.

The bulky outer coffin makes no attempt to reproduce the shape of the human body faithfully. The inner coffin, however, is a well-proportioned and fully three-dimensional image of a mummified entity standing upon a plinth and supported at the back by a pillar. The form echoes that of divine statues, and bears a striking resemblance to the figures of Ptah-Sokar-Osiris which were a common element of tomb furniture at this period. Thus here again the identification between the deity and the deceased is emphasized. The green coloring of the face is a further allusion to this divine association, since the god Osiris was regularly depicted with green flesh (green, the color of plants, symbolized new life according to ancient Egyptian thought-processes). Below the collar the sky goddess Nut spreads her wings over Shepenmehyt, and the scene of judgment and presentation to the gods, already familiar from the outer lid, is repeated on the breast. Otherwise the exterior of this coffin is dominated by blocks of inscription running vertically and laterally. These texts are written on backgrounds colored alternately red and pale yellow, a technique which helps to give emphasis to the inscriptions. On coffins of the finest quality the inscriptions are extracts from the *Book of the Dead*, perhaps selected by the prospective owner. Here, however, they are repetitious formulas—chiefly the *hetep-di-nesu* and speeches of the gods whose figures are shown – indicating that the coffin was probably bought "ready-made," fully decorated according to a standard pattern in order to reduce expense. The insides of the inner coffin are also decorated, but again in a simple style, with the *hetep-di-nesu* formula and figures of the goddess Nut drawn in black line on a white ground.

The inscriptions tell us little of Shepenmehyt beyond that fact that she was a "lady of the house" (i.e., a married woman) and that she played the sistrum to accompany rituals in the temple of Amun-Re at Thebes. X-rays of the mummy show that beneath the wrappings, is the body of an adult, who died between 25-40 years of age. Faint lines at the ends of the tibiae ("Harris lines") may testify to periods of arrested growth in earlier life. Apart from a fractured rib and a missing incisor tooth, there are no significant traces of damage to the body. There is packing in the abdomen and a large opaque mass between the thighs, which may be a bundle containing the preserved viscera. The wrappings are well-preserved and clearly show the method of retaining the outermost shroud in place by means of vertical, lateral and diagonal strips of bandage.

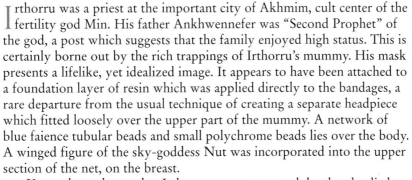

MUMMY OF IRTHORRU

EA 20745

Human remains, linen, resin, gold

From Akhmim

26th Dynasty, about 600 bc

Length 1.65 cm

Acquired in 1888

Literature: Dawson and Gray, *Mummies*, 27, pls. XIIId, XXXIIIa-c (No. 50); Taylor in Mack, *Masks. The Art of Expression*, 176, fig. 122.

Irthorru was a priest at the important city of Akhmim, cult center of the fertility god Min. His father Ankhwennefer was "Second Prophet" of the god, a post which suggests that the family enjoyed high status. This is certainly borne out by the rich trappings of Irthorru's mummy. His mask presents a lifelike, yet idealized image. It appears to have been attached to a foundation layer of resin which was applied directly to the bandages, a rare departure from the usual technique of creating a separate headpiece which fitted loosely over the upper part of the mummy. A network of blue faience tubular beads and small polychrome beads lies over the body. A winged figure of the sky-goddess Nut was incorporated into the upper section of the net, on the breast.

X-rays have shown that Irthorru was a mature adult when he died, probably between 40-50 years of age. There are lines of arrested growth on his leg-bones, possibly suggesting sickness or poor diet during childhood or adolescence, but apart from this no signs of ill-health are visible on the skeleton. The embalmers arranged his arms in a crossed position on the chest, a posture often associated with royalty in the New Kingdom but one which could also be used for private individuals, particularly in the later centuries of Egyptian history. Radiology has also shown that there is packing inside the chest, and several amulets—including a falcon-shaped pectoral and two *wedjat* eyes—are visible on the body.

Many high officials of the Late Period were buried in massive sarcophagi carved from hard stone. These costly sarcophagi were a status symbol but were also designed to frustrate the attempts of robbers to plunder the mummies.

This specimen is inscribed for a man named Pakap, who had the secondary name Wahibre-em-akhet. This "surname" incorporates the name of the pharaoh Apries, and gives a clue to the time at which Pakap lived. His titles show that he was an important official in the administration: Overseer of the cultivated lands of the south and north, Inspector of scribes, and Overseer of scribes of the king's table.

He was buried in a tomb at Giza, the largest of a group of sepulchers of the 26th Dynasty located north of the causeway of King Khafre. This tomb, without a superstructure, comprised a great shaft cut in the rock, with a burial chamber of stone blocks built at the bottom. After the burial the shaft was filled with sand, making illicit access very difficult. The mummy of Pakap was further protected by a massive outer sarcophagus and by this inner one of basalt. Although it lacks the elegant proportions of earlier mummiform coffins, it is a finely sculpted piece. The base is undecorated except for a single line of inscription on each side, mentioning Pakap's name and titles. The lid, too, is restrained in design. It is dominated by the large face framed by the striped tripartite wig which, together with the divine beard, denotes the identification of the dead man with Osiris. Below the head and the amuletic "broad collar" is a central panel of hieroglyphic text in three columns: "Recitation: the Osiris, Overseer of Scribes of the king's table Pakap, his good name being Wahibre-em-akhet, has appeared as Nefertum, as the lotus flower which is at the nose of Re. The gods will be purified at the sight of him every day." This is a passage from the *Pyramid Texts*, the oldest collection of religious writings from ancient Egypt, and it also occurred in the later *Book of the Dead* as spell 174.[1]

[1] PT utterance 249, section 266.

SARCOPHAGUS LID OF PAKAP

EA 1384

Grey basalt

From Giza (tomb LG 84; "Campbell's Tomb")

26th Dynasty, reign of Apries, 589-570 bc, or later

Length 2.60 cm; Width 1.21 cm

Literature: Porter and Moss, III 2nd ed. 290; Buhl, *Late Egyptian Anthropoid Sarcophagi*, 25 (A.6); El-Sadeek, *Twenty-Sixth Dynasty Necropolis at Gizeh*, 131, 271, pl. V; Zivie-Coche, *Giza au premier millénaire*, 283-5 and refs.

Infant mortality was high in ancient Egypt, and probably affected the families of the wealthy no less than those of the poor. During the pharaonic period relatively few children seem to have been buried with the full paraphernalia of mummification and elaborate coffins—probably because of the great expense this would have involved. In this instance, however, the child of some wealthy couple was sent into the afterlife with a finely carved wooden coffin.

In its shape and proportions this small coffin resembles the full-size anthropoid sarcophagi of the Late Period and Ptolemaic Period (see this section, object EA 1384). These were usually made of stone, and the present coffin is exceptional in being of wood. The child is adorned with the tripartite wig and wears the divine beard which proclaims that he has entered the hereafter and become assimilated with the god Osiris. A single curved line between the lappets of the wig hints at the presence of a collar which would function not merely as decoration but as a magical aid to rebirth. Although the surface of the wood has been carved with great care and skill, both the exterior and interior are completely unpainted, nor was any gesso ground laid down as a preparation for the application of paint. It can only be assumed that the mummy would have been provided with a mask and other trappings, probably made of cartonnage, on which the name and parentage of the child would have been inscribed. All that remains of the mummy is a small fragment of linen adhering to the interior of the lid.

COFFIN OF A CHILD

EA 22938

Wood

Provenance unknown

Probably early Ptolemaic Period, about 300 bc

Height 89.00 cm; Width 30.00 cm; Depth 26.00 cm

Acquired in 1890

Literature: *Art and Afterlife in Ancient Egypt*, No. 120.

29472

MUMMY MASK

EA 29472

Cartonnage, painted and gilded

Provenance unrecorded

Late Ptolemaic Period or early Roman Period, late 1st
century bc to early 1st century ad

Height 44.00 cm; Width 28.00 cm; Diameter 23.00 cm

Acquired in 1897

Literature: Andrews, *Egyptian Mummies*, 2nd ed. 35, fig. 31; *Egyptian Treasures from the British Museum* (Bowers Museum, 2000), 140-1.

A very important part of the outer trappings of a mummy was a mask, placed over the head to provide an idealized image of the deceased as a resurrected being. These masks were frequently fashioned from cartonnage, a cheap and lightweight material made from layers of linen stiffened with glue and plaster. The mask played a crucial symbolic role, for it signified the elevation of the dead person to a higher plane of existence in the afterlife. He or she was believed to attain a status of equality with the gods, and this association was conveyed in particular through the symbolic use of color and precious materials. On most mummy masks the wig was painted a uniform blue or blue-striped, and fine quality thin gold leaf was applied to the face. Religious texts assert that the gods had flesh of gold and hair made of the blue mineral lapis lazuli, so the use of blue pigment and gold leaf (or yellow paint, if funds were limited) helped by magic to transfer divinity to the wearer. In addition, the mask served as a magical protection against the loss of the head, a dreaded misfortune which it was feared might befall the unwary in the hazardous regions of the netherworld.

This mask exemplifies all the classic features of such funerary trappings. The face, collar and wig are extensively covered with gold leaf, and the wide-open eyes convey a sense of vitality and alertness—appropriate to one who has entered upon a new life. It is, however, a purely idealized image and is in no sense a true likeness of the deceased. Between the lappets of the wig are stylized floral and geometric motifs, which represent the rows of an elaborate collar. Above these are two strings of beads, one which supports an amulet in the shape of the *ankh* (sign of life). A fillet is bound around the top of the wig; it is inscribed with a funerary text and it surrounds an image of the sun god as a winged scarab beetle. Painted on the back of the mask are four mummiform deities, the *ba*-spirit of the deceased as a human-headed bird, and the sun god as a falcon. Below these is a garbled hieroglyphic inscription in seven columns, which twice repeats the name of the god Osiris but is otherwise virtually unintelligible.

FOOT CASE OF A MUMMY

EA 29475

Cartonnage, painted, gilded

Provenance unknown

Ptolemaic or Roman Period, after 305 bc

Height 20.2 cm; Width 17.5 cm; Depth 25.8 cm

Acquired in 1897

Literature: *Art and Afterlife in Ancient Egypt*, No. 71.

On many mummies of the Ptolemaic and Roman Periods the outermost wrappings were adorned with an idealized mask, a series of plaques bearing funerary texts and scenes, and a foot case—all made from cartonnage. These trappings were to some extent a substitute for a richly decorated inner coffin or cartonnage body-case; they were brilliantly painted and frequently covered with gold leaf. This foot case is typical of many that were produced at this time. The feet are represented with skin painted red, while the toenails and the sandal straps are gilded. Above each foot is a jackal representing Anubis, and the goddesses Isis and Nephthys, in attitudes of lamentation, appear at the sides. An inscription in raised relief runs along the center and is orientated so as to be legible from the head-end, i.e., it is meant to be read by the deceased.

On the base of the foot case the soles of the sandals are represented, each of which bears the figure of a foreign captive whose arms are bound around his waist with twisted papyrus-stalks. Both men are portrayed with the complexion, beard and costume associated in Egyptian art with the inhabitants of Syria-Palestine. These figures personify not only one of the traditional enemies of pharaonic Egypt, but also (on a symbolic level), the agents of chaos who were believed to pose a perpetual threat to the world-order as the Egyptians desired it to be. Through the depiction of these persons on the soles of his sandals the deceased literally trod his enemies underfoot. This triumph over the forces of evil thus ensured the continuation of cosmic order (*Maat*)—one aspect of which was the rebirth of the dead into the afterlife.

MUMMY OF A CHILD WITH PAINTED PORTRAIT

EA 21809

From Hawara (excavated by W.M. F. Petrie in 1888)

ad 40-55

Length 89 cm; Width 30.5 cm

Acquired in 1888

Literature: Petrie, *Hawara, Biahmu and Arsinoë*, 17, 42; Dawson and Gray, *Mummies*, 32, pl. XVIb (No. 60) ; Parlasca, *Ritratti di Mummie*, I, 27 (No. 7); Doxiadis, *The Mysterious Fayum Portraits*, 208 (No. 76); Corcoran, *Portrait Mummies*, 11, 20, 40; Walker and Bierbrier, *Ancient Faces*, 39-40 (No. 12); Filer in Bierbrier, *Portraits and Masks*, 123-4, pl. 46,1; Roberts in Bierbrier, *Portraits and Masks*, 21-2, pl. 23, 1.

This mummy, apparently that of a boy, was part of a group of burials found in a grave at Hawara which also comprised the bodies of two adults (one female Cairo CG 33268, the other unlocated) and those of two other children (Manchester 1769 and British Museum EA 22108). These five mummies were adorned in different styles—one of the women and this boy having painted "portraits," while the other adult and the other two children had gilded plaster masks.[1] This juxtaposition of techniques within one group led the excavator Flinders Petrie to suppose that the burials marked a point of transition from the gilt masks to panel portraits, a view which has also been adopted by later writers. Attractive as this idea may be, it is not certain; there is no firm evidence that any of these individuals were related or even that their burials took place over a limited period of time.[2]

The portrait, surrounded by layered wrappings, is executed in tempera on linen. The child is dressed in a whitish tunic and wears a red ribbon around his neck. This was probably attached to an amulet, now lost. The face is painted pink, with darker pink and ochre applied as highlights. The style of the painting, in particular the arrangement of the hair, points to a date in the reign of the Roman emperor Claudius (*ad* 41-54).

The rest of the body is covered by a painted linen shroud, adorned with rows of gilded stucco studs, and with bandages arranged in a geometrical pattern over the feet. The images on the shroud derive from long-established Egyptian models. On the breast is the sky goddess Nut, whose wings are outspread above falcon-headed and ram-headed sphinxes. At the sides and in the four compartments below are scenes of ritual, in each of which a figure in priestly costume officiates before one or more deities. The first pair of gods is obscured by the mummy wrappings, but below is (left) a priest holding a libation jar before the falcon-headed sun god and a figure wearing the double crown (probably Atum). On the right another priest recites from a papyrus scroll before Osiris. In the lower panels incense is burned and libations offered to the enthroned Osiris (left) and Re-Horakhty (right), who is protected by the winged arms of Isis and Nephthys respectively. These scenes are arranged on each side of a central band which was intended to receive an inscription, but which was in fact left blank.

Computerized tomography scans of the mummy have revealed that the body inside is that of an infant. The ribs, pelvis and thoracic spine are dislocated, damage which probably resulted from the excessively tight wrapping of the corpse by the embalmers. The scans also reveal areas of unusually high density within the bones of the legs. This may be an indication that the child suffered from a bone tumor, but it is also possible that the variable density was caused by molten resin penetrating the bones during mummification.

[1] see Roberts, pl. 23.

[2] Roberts, 22.

MUMMY MASK OF APHRODITE

EA 69020

Cartonnage, painted and gilded

From Hawara (excavated by W.M.F. Petrie in 1888)

ad 50-70

Height 53.5 cm; Width 30.8 cm

Given by H.M. Kennard to the Victoria and Albert

Museum, London in 1888; presented by the Trustees

to the British Museum in 1979

Literature: Petrie, *Hawara, Biahmu and Arsinoë*, 16-17, pl. IX, 3;
Parlasca, *Mumienporträts und Verwandte Denkmäler*, pl. 7, 4;
Grimm, *Die Römischen Mumienmasken aus Ägypten*, 49, 53, 108,
114, 117, 127 (A.6), pl. 74, 4; Walker and Bierbrier, *Ancient Faces*,
81-2 (No. 59).

The pharaonic tradition of placing an idealized mask over the head of the wrapped mummy continued during the Roman Period, when many mummies, particularly from Hawara, were provided with elaborately gilded and painted headpieces. Some of them are heavily influenced by pharaonic traditions, showing the deceased wearing a formal tripartite wig, adorned with a winged scarab motif and surrounded by vignettes showing Egyptian deities and scenes familiar from earlier funerary iconography.

Others, such as this mask of Aphrodite, daughter of Didas, show features more typical of the Roman world. She is dressed in a tunic with a purple stripe, or *clavus*, and a veil which covers her head and shoulders. This veil, however, leaves exposed Aphrodite's black hair which is arranged in rows of curls above her face, and in ringlets falling behind the ears. She is richly caparisoned with jewelry: ball-shaped earrings, a gold plaque on a necklace, showing three deities, a pair of snake-shaped bracelets, a pair of triple armlets and another pair of single armlets with a large bezel. She holds a wreath of pink flowers in her hand, an attribute found on several gilded masks of this type.

Egyptian motifs are also present but they are relegated to subordinate positions. A vulture wearing the crown of Upper Egypt is depicted on the top of the veil, its wings embracing the head, and at the back of the mask was a figure of Osiris (now mostly destroyed) accompanied by falcons and mummiform deities. Along the edge of the veil above the face is an inscription in raised relief, giving the name and parentage of the dead woman, and also her age at death, 20 years. Aphrodite's mummy was discovered by Petrie with another body, adorned in similar fashion and identified as "Souchas, brother of Didas, son of Ampholas." This man, then, may have been Aphrodite's uncle.

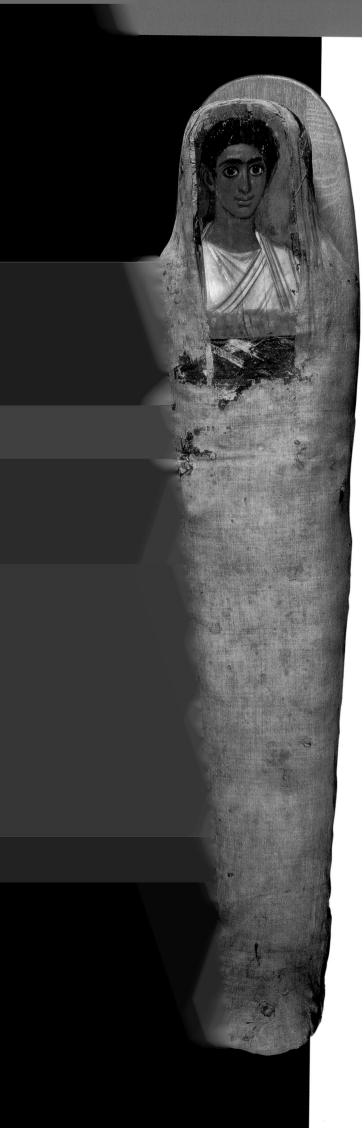

On many Egyptian mummies of the Roman period an image of the deceased was painted, either on an outer linen shroud or on to a wooden panel set into the wrappings. These "portraits" stand at the end of a long tradition in Egypt of representing the face of the deceased on the exterior of the mummy. Whereas the earlier masks were idealized, the painted panels of the Roman era are strikingly naturalistic and seem to convey an idea of the age, appearance and status of the person depicted.

The portrait panel on this mummy is executed in tempera on wood. It represents a beardless young man with curly black hair and thick eyebrows, dressed in a white tunic and mantle with a pink stripe or *clavus* visible at the left. The painter has taken care to create shading effects on the skin, using individual brush-strokes, perhaps in imitation of the more widespread encaustic technique, in which molten wax was used as a medium. The image appears to reflect the true age of the deceased, as computerized tomography scanning of the body indicates that the man died towards the end of adolescence. The skeleton is in good condition, without fractures, though there are possible signs that the deceased was already suffering from osteoarthritis. The spine is twisted, but it is uncertain whether this is a symptom of a pathological condition, such as scoliosis, or the result of manipulation of the body by the embalmers.

The mummy is wrapped in layers of cloth. Although it now appears rather plain, the portrait may originally have been set within a stuccoed and gilded outer surface, of which only small fragments now survive.[1] In the absence of any inscription, the identity of the individual is unknown, but the style of his costume and the arrangement of his hair point to a date in the mid-Antonine period, in the middle to late years of the 2nd century *ad*. Although it has been stated to come from Memphis, there is no firm evidence for this. Since it formed part of the first collection of the British consul Henry Salt, the mummy is more likely to have been found at Thebes, where many of Salt's antiquities were obtained; three "Greek" mummies with wooden "masks" were found by Salt's collecting agent d'Athanasi in a tomb at Gurnet Murai on the Theban West Bank in 1821.[2]

[1] Corcoran, *Portrait Mummies*, 12, No. 23, lists it among "stucco-shrouded mummies".

[2] d'Athanasi, *Researches*, 100-1.

MUMMY OF A MAN
WITH PORTRAIT PANEL

EA 6713

Possibly from Thebes

Roman Period, about ad 140-180

Acquired from the first collection of

Henry Salt in 1823

Literature: Dawson and Gray, *Mummies*, 30, pl. XVb (No.
56); Parlasca, *Ritratti di Mummie* II, 87, Tav 116, 1 (477);
Walker and Bierbrier, *Ancient Faces*, 118-119 (No. 115);
Filer in Bierbrier, *Portraits and Masks*, 122, pl. 44, 1-2.

EA 22374

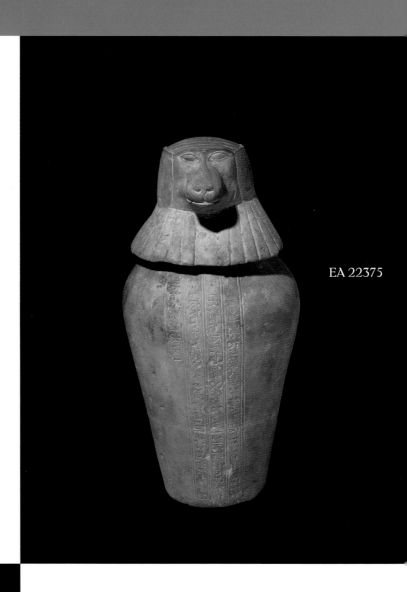

EA 22375

EA 22376

EA 22377

The internal organs extracted from the chest of the body during mummification were made into four packages. Each nominally contained one specific part of the anatomy: liver, lungs, stomach and intestines. These organs were preserved using natron salts, oils and resins before being wrapped in linen. They thus were treated as though each was a miniature mummy, and indeed in elaborate burials each organ pack was sometimes provided with a miniature mummy-mask or placed inside a small-scale anthropoid coffin.

However, the usual procedure was to place the organ packages into four jars, which were placed in the tomb close to the coffin. Now known as "Canopic" jars (after a spurious association with the Delta town of Canopus, where Osiris is said to have been worshipped in the form of a vase-shaped image), they first appeared at the height of the Old Kingdom and continued in use (with some interruptions) until the end of the Late Period. The four organs were placed under the protection of the Four Sons of Horus. These deities, whose names were Imsety, Hapy, Duamutef and Qebehsenuef, are invoked in inscriptions on the jars to give protection. Early examples had lids in the form of human heads, but beginning about 1400 *bc* each lid depicted the guardian genius with a distinctive head: a man for Imsety, a baboon for Hapy, a jackal for Duamutef and a falcon for Qebehsenuef.

This set of jars is inscribed for a man named Djedbastetiufankh, who held many sacerdotal offices including that of priest of the goddess Neith. They were found by Flinders Petrie in a tomb at Hawara. It was a family grave, and Petrie also discovered a second set of jars, almost identical to these and again inscribed for a Djedbastetiufankh. Both men held the same titles and had the same father, Horwedja, but were born of different mothers—in this case the mother was Ankhet. The jars have unusually long and detailed inscriptions, in which the Sons of Horus are concerned not so much to protect the body parts inside, but to assure the deceased that he will have food and drink in the afterlife.

CANOPIC JARS OF DJEDBASTETIUFANKH

EA 22374

EA 22375

EA 22376

EA 22377

Limestone

From Hawara

30th Dynasty

Height (all jars) 49.5 cm

Acquired in 1889

Literature: Porter and Moss, IV, 102; Petrie, *Hawara, Biahmu and Arsinoë*, 8-9, 23, pl. IV; British Museum, *A Guide to the First and Second Egyptian Rooms*, 2nd ed. 125-6; Budge, *The Mummy*, 2nd ed. 244-5.

The four packages of viscera were not always placed in canopic jars. Depending on the fashion of burial customary at the time, they might be put back into the body cavity or enclosed within a wooden chest. Canopic containers of the Late and Ptolemaic Periods were often constructed and decorated in imitation of shrines. The intention was to convey divine status by association—ust as the principal function of a shrine was to house the physical embodiment of a god, so the shrine-shaped box implied that whatever lay inside possessed the attributes of divinity, including regenerative powers and everlastingness.

This chest is inscribed for a man named Irthorru, who held both religious and secular offices at Thebes. He was a "Great and efficient singer in the necropolis," a scribe and a priest of Amun in the temple of Karnak.

A wooden figure was originally mounted on the lid. Only the dowel-holes for its attachment and the silhouette of the object can now be seen, but by comparison with other, better-preserved specimens, it was probably a falcon. On the front of the box is painted with a *djed* pillar, symbolizing the god Osiris. It is provided not only with his distinctive crown but also with human arms grasping royal scepters. This image is balanced on the back by the *tit*, emblem of Isis, the sister-wife of Osiris. On the sides are the Sons of Horus: baboon-headed Hapy and human-headed Imsety on the right, Qebehsenuef and Duamutef (here with the heads of a jackal and a falcon, respectively) on the left. The hieroglyphic texts by their sides state that they will grant various benefits to Irthorru, including life and protection, while Imsety promises that "your corpse will be uninjured, your limbs beautiful."

Four rudimentary hinges, painted on the front, are a reminder that in reality such a shrine would be provided with double doors, but to open this small-scale replica the top must be removed. The interior is unpainted and contains only one cavity. The original contents have long since disappeared but drops of solidified black resin indicate that the chest held one or more bundles, probably containing the embalmed internal organs of the deceased.

CANOPIC CHEST OF IRTHORRU

EA 8535

Sycamore fig, painted

Probably from Thebes

Ptolemaic Period, 305-30 bc

Height 56 cm; Weight 24.2 cm

Literature: *Art and Afterlife in Ancient Egypt*, No. 68.

FIGURES OF THE SONS OF HORUS

EA 8389

EA 15569

Clay coated with beeswax

Provenance unknown

Third Intermediate Period, about 1070-664 bc

Height 9.0 cm; Width 3.0 cm

Height 7.6 cm; Width 3.0 cm

Acquired in 1839

Acquired in 1879

(Anastasi Collection)

Literature: *Art and Afterlife in Ancient Egypt*, No. 65. For these figures in general, see Taylor, *Death and Afterlife*, 72-3.

During the Third Intermediate Period, the treatment of the internal organs of the mummy changed. Instead of being placed in canopic jars, each of the four principal organs (liver, lungs, stomach and intestines) was wrapped in a separate linen package and replaced inside the mummy's chest before the body was wrapped. This may have been a response to a heightened concern to preserve the integrity of the corpse. Pressures on Egypt's economy in these years meant that few elaborate tombs were built, and cemeteries were "managed" more rigorously, resulting in mummies being moved from tomb to tomb. Under these circumstances, the vital organs might become separated from the body if stored in separate containers.

The protection of the Four Sons of Horus, formerly conveyed through the iconography of the canopic jars and through their inscriptions, was now assured through the use of figurines of the deities, one of which was included in each package containing part of the viscera. Most of these statuettes represented the gods in mummy shape, though occasionally they were depicted as living beings. In the majority of cases, these figures were made entirely or partly from beeswax. This substance was believed by the ancient Egyptians to hold magical properties, and the wax used for these images was deliberately colored to add to their symbolic effectiveness. These colors included black, white, yellow and (as in these examples) red, probably to invoke the regenerative power of the sun god.

4

TRAPPINGS OF THE
MUMMY

The process of mummification was intended to transform the corruptible corpse into a new, eternal body endowed with supernatural qualities. This mysterious procedure was to be achieved partly through purging the corpse of its corruption products and replacing them with divine substances such as resins and oils. In addition, the placing of objects of magical significance on the body or in close proximity to it was believed to be of great importance. Some of these items played a part in defining the new character of the body as a *sah*-image: these included the gilded mask on the head, and the gold or silver stalls placed over the fingers and toes. Besides these, many other objects were placed on the body to magically confirm the status of the dead and to equip them with special powers.

Mummies of royal persons were the most richly adorned. The unwrapping of the mummy of Tutankhamun brought to light lavish jewelry and pharaonic insignia. From this and from other royal burials it is known that diadems, kilts with decorative belts and aprons, and gold sandals were placed on kings' mummies from at least the 17th to the 22nd Dynasty. Tutankhamun was also equipped with the kingly scepters, the crook and flail. This concentration of precious materials made the royal mummies targets for tomb robbers, and consequently very few unplundered royal burials have come to light in modern times.

The bodies of non-royal persons were generally less richly adorned with jewelry, but many objects of magical significance were provided, nonetheless. The majority of these were amulets. Amulets played an important part in Egyptian religious attitudes from an early period. Broadly defined, an amulet acted as a medium through which supernatural power or attributes could be conveyed to a person, either living or dead. The amulet might be a natural object such as a shell or a man-made item.

In ancient Egypt a wide range of objects were believed to possess magical qualities. They were often used in life to give protection against disease or the hazards of childbirth. In the funerary sphere they were used for many purposes: to safeguard the integrity of the corpse, to give protection against harmful forces, to endow the owner with possessions and to equip the owner with special powers (particularly the qualities of gods).

Many amulets were small images made from stone, semi-precious stone, metal, faience, glass, ceramic or wood. Their power was believed to reside in their shape, their color, and the material from which they were made. Gold, for example, conferred divine status and everlasting life, while the color green was associated with plants and, by extension, with the idea of the renewal of life.

Several important funerary amulets are described and illustrated in the *Book of the Dead*, together with instructions for their use. Besides specifying the form and the material of which the amulet was to be made, the texts explained where it should be placed on the body and what words should be recited over it to bring it into effectiveness.

The placing of amulets within the wrappings of mummies began to be common in the First Intermediate Period, when simple images of gods and parts of the human body were fashioned. In the New Kingdom the number of amulets began to increase. The most important were the *djed* pillar and *tit*, heart amulet and heart scarab. The heart scarab was related to the judgment of the deceased, and was inscribed with a spell to prevent the heart from testifying against its owner in the tribunal of the gods. This basic range of amulets was greatly expanded in the 1st millennium *bc*. Many small images in stone and faience were placed between the layers of bandages, particularly on the throat and chest, traditionally regarded as the most vulnerable areas of the body. Scarabs, *wedjat* eyes, *djed* pillars and images of deities were among the most common. In the Late and Ptolemaic Periods the amulets were laid out in carefully composed schemes; sometimes there were two layers of amulets in the wrappings of one mummy.

Items of bodily adornment could also function as amulets. This was particularly true of collars and rings, which often had bezels in the forms of amulets. Some amulets were threaded on to bracelets and strings and placed at the neck or around the arms. It was not always necessary for such items to be placed on the mummy; hence some pieces of jewelry have been discovered in tombs inside the coffin or in separate boxes. Certain objects of amuletic significance, however, such as the hypocephalus, had to be located in close proximity to the corpse in order for them to function effectively. On account of this, they have usually been found directly beneath the head of the deceased.

Literature:
Andrews, *Amulets of Ancient Egypt*; Taylor, *Death and the Afterlife*, 200-7.

PAIR OF SANDAL SOLES FOR A MUMMY

EA 26779

Leather, painted and gilded

From Saqqara

Ptolemaic Period, 305-30 bc

Length 21.00 cm

Acquired in 1891

Besides their practical function, sandals were regarded as important symbolic items for the adornment of the blessed dead. They were placed on or near the mummy in the burial chamber, to enable the deceased to leave the tomb at will and to tread his enemies underfoot. Both real sandals and replicas have been found in many burials from the Old and Middle Kingdoms, while images of them were painted on the walls of tombs and the surfaces of coffins. In the Late and Ptolemaic Periods it was more usual for the shape of the sandal soles to be painted on the cartonnage foot cases of mummies. An alternative to this custom was to fashion individual soles, which would then be bound to the mummy's feet using strips of linen.

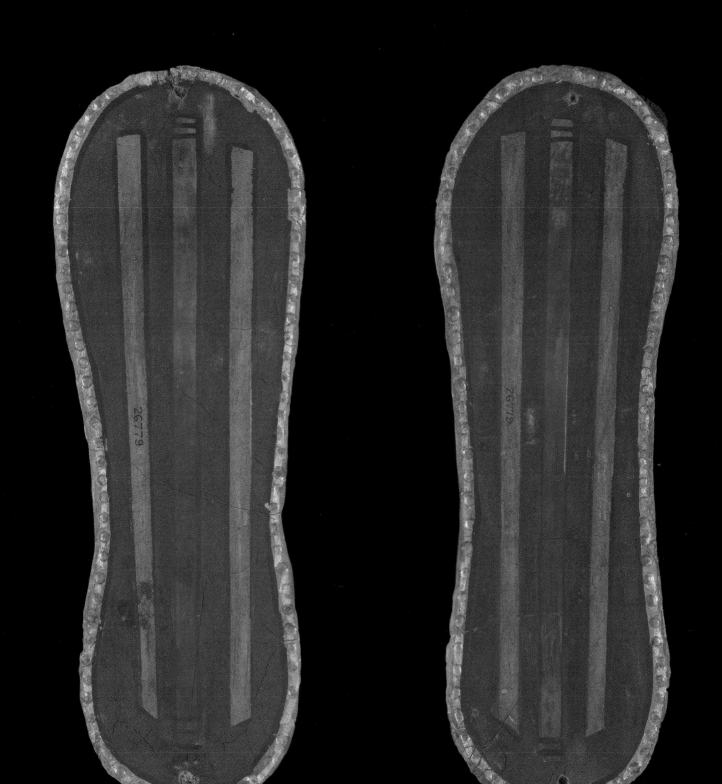

A disc of linen (occasionally papyrus or bronze) known as a hypocephalus was a feature of the trappings of elite mummies in the Ptolemaic Period. These objects were covered with inscriptions and images which relate to one of the last spells in the *Book of the Dead*, spell 162. The purpose of the text was to kindle a life-giving fire beneath the head of the dead person. The spell was supposed to be recited over an amulet representing a cow. This was to be placed on the mummy's throat, and a drawing of it on papyrus placed under his head. Probably these instructions gave rise to the practice, in the Late Period, of placing a disc of linen with appropriate texts and images, beneath the mummy's head.

These discs display various images, not all of which are readily understandable, and unfortunately the brief texts which sometimes appear do not explain their precise meaning. This example includes elements typical of hypocephali. At top is a two-headed deity in human form who holds a scepter on which is the image of the jackal-god Wepwawet. Two gods appear in boats: on the left is a falcon with outspread wings, and on the right is a mummiform falcon-headed figure clearly recognizable as the sun god wearing the solar disc as his headdress. The scarab beetle, another manifestation of the sun, is depicted in front of him. In the next register the god Amun-Re is depicted as a mummiform deity with four ram-heads, adored by pairs of baboons. Rotating the disc one hundred and eighty degrees, one sees another scene, in which a cow is the principal figure, facing the Four Sons of Horus and a scarab beetle. The cow, at least, can be clearly related to spell 162, which is put into the mouth of an *ihet*-cow, there described as the mother of Re. Behind the cow is a female figure whose head is the *wedjat* eye within a disc, and a seated figure with upraised arm who faces a serpent with human legs (this part of the object is partially damaged).

Hypocephali were not widely used, and seem to have been mainly restricted to the burials of certain priestly families in Upper Egypt. This example was made for a woman named Neshorpakhered, who was a Sistrum-player of Amun-Re.

HYPOCEPHALUS

EA 36188

Plaster on linen, ink

From Thebes

Late-early Ptolemaic Period, 4th-3rd century bc

Diameter 14.00 cm

Acquired from the collection of Robert Hay

Literature: Quirke and Spencer, *The British Museum Book of Ancient Egypt*, 96, fig. 75; *Art and Afterlife in Ancient Egypt*, No. 70.

LARGE BLUE SCARAB

EA 30050

Faience

Provenance unknown

Late Period

Width 11.40 cm; Length 17.30 cm

Acquired in 1898

Unpublished. See Friedman, *Gifts of the Nile* for the meanings and uses of faience; Grimm, *Die Römischen Mumienmasken aus Ägypten* for some examples of mummy-masks with scarabs on their heads, and Arnold, *Encyclopaedia of Ancient Egyptian Architecture,* 20-1 for an overview of ceramics in construction. For the specific example of Medinet Habu, see Hölscher, *The excavation of Medinet Habu* IV, 38-47, compare pl. 37-8.

This large faience scarab has been, in design terms, simplified down to the essential elements. The elytra (wing cases) are indicated in incised detail, as are the prothorax, head and clypeus in very simple terms, but the legs are not shown. The purpose for which it was made is uncertain, but it is far too large to have any amuletic significance. Some metallic corrosion has been noted on the underside, which suggests that it may have been attached to a metal base, perhaps some form of mount.

Two possibilities suggest themselves for its original purpose. Certain mummy-masks of the Graeco-Roman period bear a scarab of faience placed on top of the head, alluding to the role of the sun god in the deceased's afterlife. These tend to be smaller than this example, but would also explain the traces of the mount.

Another possibility is that it was an "architectural ceramic," mounted into a wall scene, either in a temple or perhaps a palace, as an elaborate inlay. Ceramics of various types, including pieces of faience (although nothing quite like this example) were set into the sunk relief of the decoration of Medinet Habu and a number of other New Kingdom temples or palaces. An unpublished example has been noted in the Cairo Museum (JE 46356) of a large lapis-lazuli scarab set into silver, with wings of gold inlaid with semi-precious stones. It was clearly attached to a flat surface, and is probably also of the Ptolemaic Period.

The Egyptian word for faience was *tjehenet.* The brilliant blue, the most common color of faience, was closely linked with the symbolism of new life and rebirth. The luminosity of the material can also be associated with the sun god, and of course the symbolic value in the present object is thereby doubled, as the scarab is the solar symbol *par excellence.*

The papyrus-column amulet is known in Egyptian as
wadj. The body of this example is plain green without
further decoration, and has a pierced suspension ring at the
top. Green fresh plant life represented youthfulness, new
life and rebirth to the Egyptians, and the presence of this
particular amulet on the body was to ensure that the
deceased remained forever young, and was not injured.
Book of the Dead spell 159 consists of a spell to be spoken
over a papyrus-column of green feldspar set on the throat
of the deceased; spell 160 is related and says "To me
belongs a papyrus-column of green feldspar which is not
imperfect, and which the hand of Thoth supports, for he
detests injury. If it is intact, then I will be hale; if it is uninjured, then will I be uninjured; if it is not struck, then I will
not be struck. It is what Thoth has said which knits your
spine together."

This example is made of faience rather than feldspar, as
are most known examples. Faience was doubtless a more
reasonably-priced material than stone, and the classic
green/blue color of faience made it a very suitable material
for a substitute. Recent computerized tomography scans of
the mummy of Nesperennub in the British Museum have
revealed a papyrus scepter amulet on his breast.

PAPYRUS COLUMN AMULET

EA 7445

Faience

Provenance unknown

Probably Third Intermediate Period or Late Period

Length 5.2 cm; Diameter 1.6 cm

Acquired from the collection of Joseph Sams in 1834

Literature: *Art and Afterlife in Ancient Egypt,* No 90. Translation of Book of the
Dead, Faulkner, *Book of the Dead,* 155.

This funerary amulet takes the form of the head of a cobra with deflated hood. Called in Egyptian *menqe-byt,* this form of amulet was first depicted inside the coffins of officials dating to the Middle Kingdom, among the so called "object friezes," although not, unfortunately, on the object friezes of the coffin of Seni in this exhibit. Along the back of the head of this example is a space left for adding a text, which was never cut.

The primary purpose of the snake head amulet was probably to ward off snakebites, which were feared by both the dead and the living; spell 34 of the *Book of the Dead* contains a spell to this end. However, the name of the amulet, linked with the words for "fan" and "coolness," suggests it might also have been intended to provide cool refreshment to the throat; it has a loop for suspension, so it would be worn at the neck.

Actual snake head amulets are first known from the New Kingdom, and are made from various materials. Examples from the royal burials of Thutmose IV and Tutankhamun in the Valley of the Kings are made of faience, whitish stone, and wood. There are many examples in museum collections for which provenance has not been determined, most of which probably came from private collections. Infrequently, examples are found which bear inscriptions, such as that of Khay in the British Museum, dating to the reign of Ramesses II (exhibited in the Bowers Museum in 2000); a small number have actually been found in the course of excavations, such as one from the tomb of Aperia, the vizier of Akhenaten, buried at Saqqara, one from the 19th Dynasty tomb of Nefersekheru at Thebes, and a couple from a 19th Dynasty burial of an Apis bull in the Serapeum at Saqqara. These non-royal examples tend to be made of red stones or glass. Complementing the latter, three pictures of such amulets are known from the walls of Theban tombs 96, 99 and 79, from the reigns of Thutmose III and Amenhotep II.

SNAKE HEAD AMULET

EA 3128

Red jasper

Provenance unknown

New Kingdom

Length 4.93 cm; Width 1.87 cm; Depth 1.41 cm

Literature: Andrews, *Amulets of Ancient Egypt,* p.84. Compare the example in *Egyptian Treasures* (Bowers Museum 2000, 122-3).

EA 27385

Schist

Provenance unknown

Probably New Kingdom

Height 1.78 cm; Width 4.21 cm; Length 6.59 cm

Acquired in 1896

This green heart scarab is of a more unusual type. Instead of the stone actually being modeled into the shape of the beetle, the oval is decorated on the upper side with a raised relief representation of a scarab, its elytra marked with a double suture. Both upper and lower sides are curved; the bottom is inscribed with eight lines of hieroglyphs with *Book of the Dead* spell 30 for a man named Amenhotep. The ledge at the top in some examples is pierced so it could be used for a suspension thread.

EA 7965

Serpentinite

Provenance unknown

Probably New Kingdom

Height 2.65 cm; Width 4.19 cm; Length 5.95 cm

Uninscribed heart-scarab, with striated elytra, unpierced. In shape it is not unlike EA 7899 opposite.

HEART SCARABS

According to ancient Egyptian beliefs, the heart was the most important of the internal organs: it alone was the seat of intelligence, and a repository of memory. Because of this the heart was the only internal organ left in place during the embalming process. As it retained the memory of its owner's deeds on earth it would be weighed symbolically in the balance in the underworld to ascertain its owner's worthiness to enter the Egyptian version of paradise. This scene of weighing the heart is found in almost all *Book of the Dead* papyri and also in painting and relief.

Should the heart be destroyed, the Egyptians, as always, had an inventive and convenient solution: an amulet in its shape could act as a substitute. In addition, as here, many heart amulets bear the so-called heart scarab formula (spell 30B of the *Book of the Dead*) which, during the weighing, bound the heart to silence about its owner's earthly misdeeds. The spells usually found on a heart amulet are designed to prevent the heart being taken away from its owner, or, if such a dire event should happen, to return it to the deceased.

The classic heart scarab is 3-10 cm in length, and made of a black or green stone. A typical text is that on EA 27385 opposite, the beginning of which reads: "Heart of my mother! Heart of my mother! Heart of my (different) forms! Do not stand against me as a witness or against me in the tribunal; do not come against me in the presence of the supervisor of the balance."

The heart scarab is best known from the New Kingdom, although the earliest examples are perhaps of the 13th Dynasty. Not all were inscribed (see EA 7965 opposite). From the 25th Dynasty onwards smaller uninscribed scarabs appear among the various amulets placed in the mummy wrappings, and a winged variety appears in conjunction with bead nets. Unlike the much smaller scarabs which were perhaps worn in life and used as seals, known from the First Intermediate Period onwards, the majority of heart scarabs were not pierced for suspension or attachment.

Literature:
Andrews, *Amulets of Ancient Egypt*, 56-9; Taylor, *Death and the Afterlife*, 205-6.

EA 7899

Basalt

Provenance unknown

Probably 19th Dynasty

Height 2.14 cm; Width 4.05 cm; Length 5.57 cm

Acquired from the collection of Joseph Sams in 1834

In this heart-scarab of Iny the elytra (wing-cases) are marked with a double suture. The scarab is unpierced, and the base is inscribed with nine lines of white painted hieroglyphs from *Book of the Dead* spell 30.

EA 38073

Basalt

Provenance unknown

18th Dynasty (early)

Height 1.85 cm; Width 4.08 cm; Length 6.79 cm

Literature: *Art and Afterlife in Ancient Egypt*, No. 76; Andrews, *Amulets of Ancient Egypt*, fig.44; Shaw & Nicholson, *British Museum Dictionary*, p.123.

This black heart-scarab has a human face at the front. The elytra are marked with a double suture. It is unpierced, and the base is inscribed with nine lines of hieroglyphs with *Book of the Dead* spell 30 for a woman named Aset (Isis).

This amulet represents the index and middle fingers with nails of a left human hand. Such amulets are always made of a black material and occur in the burials of the Late Period only. Black is the color of the jackal-headed god Anubis, and also one of the colors associated with Osiris—in this case representing the black fertile soil which gave new life to Egypt and by extension to the dead.

The amulet's most common position on the mummy is adjacent to the embalming incision, through which the internal organs of the body were removed. Thus a favored explanation of its purpose is that it represents the fingers of the embalmer, or perhaps those of the god Anubis who oversaw the act of embalmment, and thus it could by magical means reconfirm the process of embalming. It could also have afforded protection to this vulnerable part of the mummy and helped keep any dangerous influences away from the embalmed body.

TWO FINGER AMULET

EA 8362

Steatite

Provenance unknown

Late Period

Length 9.2 cm; Width 2.8 cm; Thickness 1.3 cm

Acquired from the collection of Joseph Sams in 1834

Unpublished. Compare Andrews, *Amulets*, 85, and a similar object which came to the Bowers Museum in 2000: *Egyptian Treasures*, 128-9.

8362.

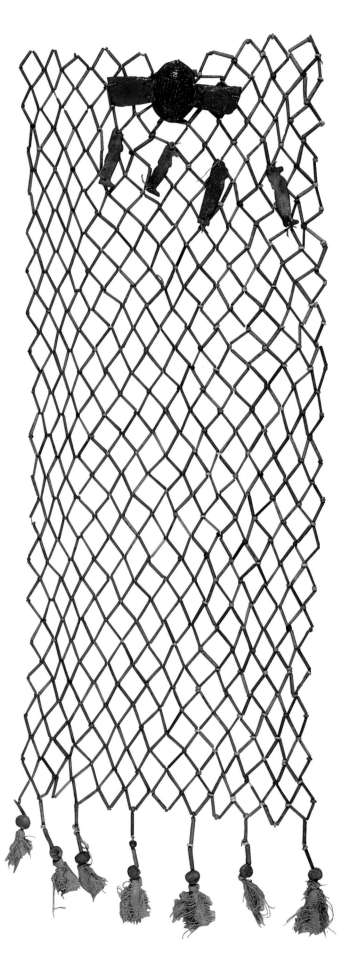

EA 18246
Faience
From Thebes
Length 57.00 cm (not including tassels); Width 23.50 cm
Acquired in 1887

Rectangular section of a net of faience beads, comprising short cylinder beads of red, yellow, blue and white, some strung in pairs, and blue standard cylinder beads, some of which are faded, strung in a lozenge-pattern. One end is embellished with seven tassels, each comprising a short white cylinder, a blue-green standard cylinder and red or blue globular beads with frayed fiber tassels. Into the net are incorporated a blue winged scarab and four pale blue sons of Horus amulets, also of faience.

BEAD NETS AND ASSOCIATED AMULETS

There were a number of significant changes in the burial equipment of well-to-do Egyptians in the later part of the Third Intermediate Period. Along with changes to coffin decoration and the introduction of a new vaulted coffin type, the Egyptians introduced bead nets and their associated amulets.

A net of faience beads, as typified by EA 18246 opposite, had occasionally been seen in earlier interments, but now it became an essential part of the burial. The symbolic function of the bead net was to evoke the god Osiris and stress the assimilation of the dead person with that god. It is believed that the association with that deity goes back to a net-like garment placed over the robe of Osiris which is seen in tomb depictions from at least the New Kingdom. The blue coloring of the beads also suggests a link with the sky and hence the protection of Nut. At roughly the same time as the bead net appeared, a custom was also developed of employing a special set of five amulets for the mummy, in addition to other amulets which had been placed on the body for many years. Four of these were the Sons of Horus, usually in the form of plain roughly shaped pieces of faience, and the fifth was a winged scarab, also usually made of faience with separate body and wings. These amulets stressed the protection offered by the Sons of Horus, genii perhaps best known for their association with canopic jars, and also the assimilation of the deceased with the sun as indicated by the scarab. The amulets could be sewn directly on to the mummy wrappings or incorporated into the stringing of the bead net. A variation soon developed, in which these five amulets were themselves "woven" out of beads and incorporated into the net (see EA 90084 below). Bead nets from the Late and Ptolemaic Periods sometimes incorporate additional protective figures of deities such as Isis and Nephthys.

Both Unpublished:
See Taylor, *Death and Afterlife*, 206-7 for comments on bead nets. See Silvano, *Egitto e vicino oriente* 3 (1980), 83-97 for a typology.

EA 90084

Colored faience

Provenance unknown

Late Period, 664-305 bc

Height 10.6 cm; Width 22.6 cm

In the Late Period it became the fashion for mummies of the wealthy to be adorned with a network of beads. Into these nets were often woven figures of deities. These might be molded in faience or made up as mosaics of small beads of different colors. This scarab beetle is an example of the latter method, being composed of small beads of red, yellow, blue, green and black, set within a net of blue tubular beads (a few of which remain beneath the left wing). The beetle is depicted with outspread wings, and solar discs are shown between the front and back legs. It is a common image of the sun god at dawn, a powerful symbol of rebirth and new life, and one which appeared with great frequency on the lids of coffins and on other trappings of the mummy.

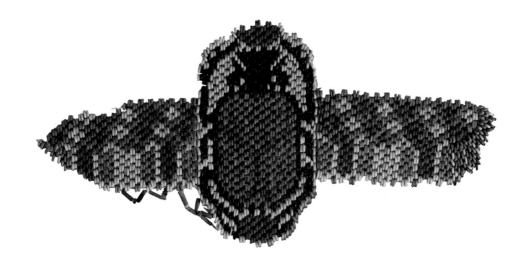

GIRDLE OF ISIS AMULET

EA 20639

Red jasper

Provenance unknown

Later New Kingdom, perhaps c. 1250-1100 bc

Length 6.5 cm; Width 2.6 cm; Thickness 0.60 cm

Acquired from the Anastasi Collection in 1857

Literature: *Egyptian Treasures* (Bowers Museum 2000): 116-117. Shaw & Nicholson, *British Museum Dictionary*, 299. Translation of *Book of the Dead*, Faulkner, *Book of the Dead*, 155.

This funerary amulet is known as a *tit*, and takes the shape of an open loop of red jasper from the bound lower end of which hangs a long sash flanked by two folded loops; there is a ribbed tube for suspension at the top. Some examples are inscribed—this one bears the name of a man called Nefer. The amulet is supposed to take the form of the girdle of Isis, the spouse of Osiris, and she would protect the deceased.

Spell 156 of the *Book of the Dead* prescribes that such amulets should be made of red jasper, as here, which is the color of the blood of the goddess Isis. Placed on the neck of the mummy it would afford the body the protection of the goddess: "You have your blood, O Isis; you have your power, O Isis; you have your magic, O Isis. The amulet is a protection for the Great One which will drive away whoever would commit crime against him."

In addition to jasper, other red stones could be used, or indeed glass (Tutankhamun had such an amulet in his tomb). After the New Kingdom, examples in faience became more common, presumably largely on the basis of cost, although the association of faience, particularly the green and blue varieties, with resurrection should not be overlooked.

FIGURINE OF THOTH

EA 11344

Faience

Provenance unknown

Probably 26th Dynasty, 664-525 bc

Height 10.5 cm; Width 2.2 cm; Depth 3.7 cm

Acquired in 1879

Thoth, the god of wisdom and patron of scribes, possessed two animal manifestations: those of a baboon and an ibis. He features prominently in funerary scenes, recording the outcome of the weighing of the heart and assisting Horus in the revivification and purification of Osiris. This faience amulet is typical of many which were placed within the wrappings of mummies in the Late Period. It represents Thoth in his ibis-headed form, wearing a kilt and a striated wig. These figures were usually positioned on the mummy's chest, forming part of a row of protective deities.

The Egyptian name for a headrest amulet is *weres*. It has a characteristically long narrow base, cylindrical support and curved neck rest. Such amulets were usually made of polished haematite. The black color of that stone could be symbolically associated with the black earth of the land after the inundation, and hence with Osiris and hopes for regeneration, new life and rebirth.

The primary purpose of the headrest amulet was to raise the head of the dead in resurrection. The Egyptians may have associated this symbolically with the rising of the sun in the morning—some have seen a parallel between the curve of the headrest and the hieroglyph of the horizon where the sun rose. According to spell 166 of the *Book of the Dead,* the headrest amulet had two roles. Besides raising the head of the deceased in regeneration, it prevented the head being taken away:

> "May the pigeons awaken you when you are asleep, O <name>, may they awaken your head at the horizon. Raise yourself, so that you may be triumphant over what was done against you, for Ptah has felled your enemies, and it is commanded that action be taken against those who would harm you … Your head shall not be taken from you afterwards, your head shall not be taken from you for ever."

Some headrests, although not this one, are actually inscribed with this spell. The headrest amulet might also have been intended to act as a substitute for an actual headrest. One of the earliest such amulets is from the tomb of Tutankhamun and is made of iron, although in that tomb there were also several regular headrests. In the first part of the Third Intermediate Period further iron examples were placed on the mummies buried in the royal tombs at Tanis. Only in the late Third Intermediate Period and Late Period did these amulets (then of haematite) come into use for non-royal persons.

HEADREST AMULET

EA 12001

Highly polished Haematite

Probably Late Third Intermediate Period or Late Period, after 750 bc

Height 1.9 cm; Length 2.7 cm; Thickness 1.2 cm

Literature: *Art and Afterlife in Ancient Egypt*, No. 81. Translation of Book of the Dead, Faulkner, *Book of the Dead*, 161.

DJED PILLAR AMULET

EA 12196

Faience

Late Period, c. 600 bc or later

Length 9.4 cm; Width 2.9 cm; Thickness 1.3 cm

Donated by Lt. Gen. Augustus W.H. Meyrick in 1878

Literature: *Art and Afterlife in Ancient Egypt*, No. 88. Translation of Book of the Dead, Faulkner, *Book of the Dead,* 155. See further Andrews, *Amulets,* 82-3. See Taylor, *Mummy: the inside story,* for the mummy of Nesperennub.

The *djed* pillar takes the form of the hieroglyph which means "enduring" or "stable," and it would thus confer these qualities on the owner of the amulet. It came to be particularly associated with Osiris, god of the dead, and was considered to represent his stylized backbone and ribs. Its value as an amulet was that it would give the deceased person the stability of Osiris and would allow him or her to stand upright in the next life. Spell 155 of the *Book of the Dead* is a magical spell to be recited over a *djed* pillar placed over the throat of the deceased on the day of burial: "Raise yourself, O Osiris, place yourself on your side, that I may put water beneath you and that I may bring you a *djed* pillar of gold so you may rejoice at it." Examples of this amulet have been found in varying places on mummies, although the most recent examination of a mummy in the British Museum by advanced 3D technology has shown that the *djed* amulet of the priest Nesperennub was indeed on his throat.

Although this spell was prescribed for a *djed* pillar of gold, few surviving examples are made of that material, probably because gold amulets were beyond the means of most private individuals. The majority are of green/blue faience, and occasionally bear traces of having been gilded. Faience, predominantly but by no means exclusively blue or green in color, was a material particularly associated with the symbolism of new life and resurrection, and was an appropriate substitute.

Perhaps originally the *djed* represented a stylized tree-trunk with lopped-off branches. It may have been associated in the Old Kingdom with Sokar, the funerary god of the Memphite necropolis. There was a ritual "raising the *djed* pillar" in which a large *djed* was apparently pulled upright by ropes. This ritual had certainly entered the Osiride sphere by the Middle Kingdom, and came to be seen as a representation of the victory of Osiris over his enemies. Hence the amulet could, as with so many Egyptian symbols, have multiple and complex significance.

EA 26300

Faience

Third Intermediate Period

Length 8.9 cm; Width 7.2 cm; Thickness 1.00 cm

Acquired in 1895

A wedjat eye of polychrome faience: the eye and the highly stylized eyebrow are of blue faience, while the area between the angled bar of the eye and the eye itself is filled with red faience. The cornea and iris are white and black respectively. Some of the larger examples of such amulets exhibit ornate decoration in the exaggerated area between the eye and the eyebrow; in the present instance there are three rows of tiny cats. This large amulet required two rings for suspension at the top.

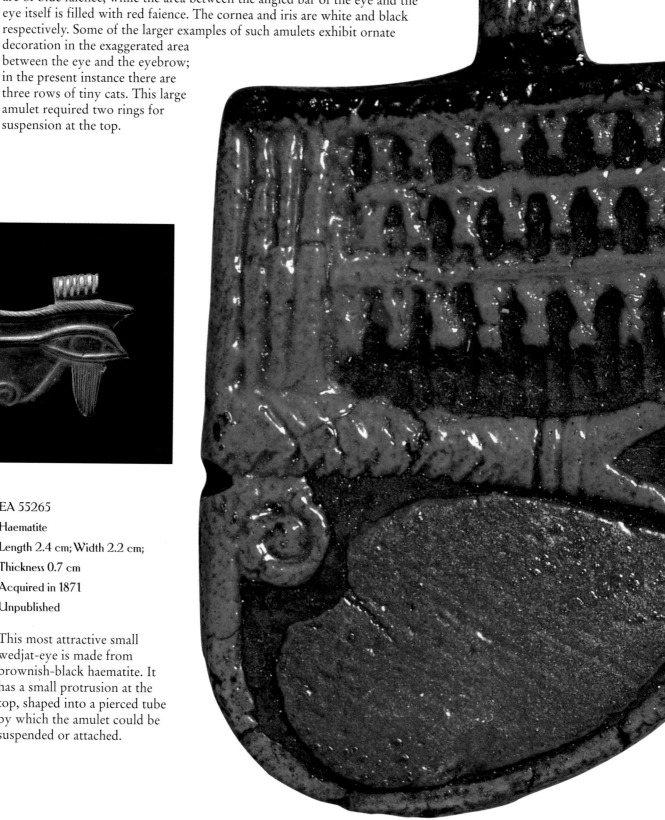

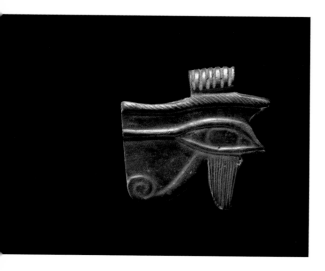

EA 55265

Haematite

Length 2.4 cm; Width 2.2 cm; Thickness 0.7 cm

Acquired in 1871

Unpublished

This most attractive small wedjat-eye is made from brownish-black haematite. It has a small protrusion at the top, shaped into a pierced tube by which the amulet could be suspended or attached.

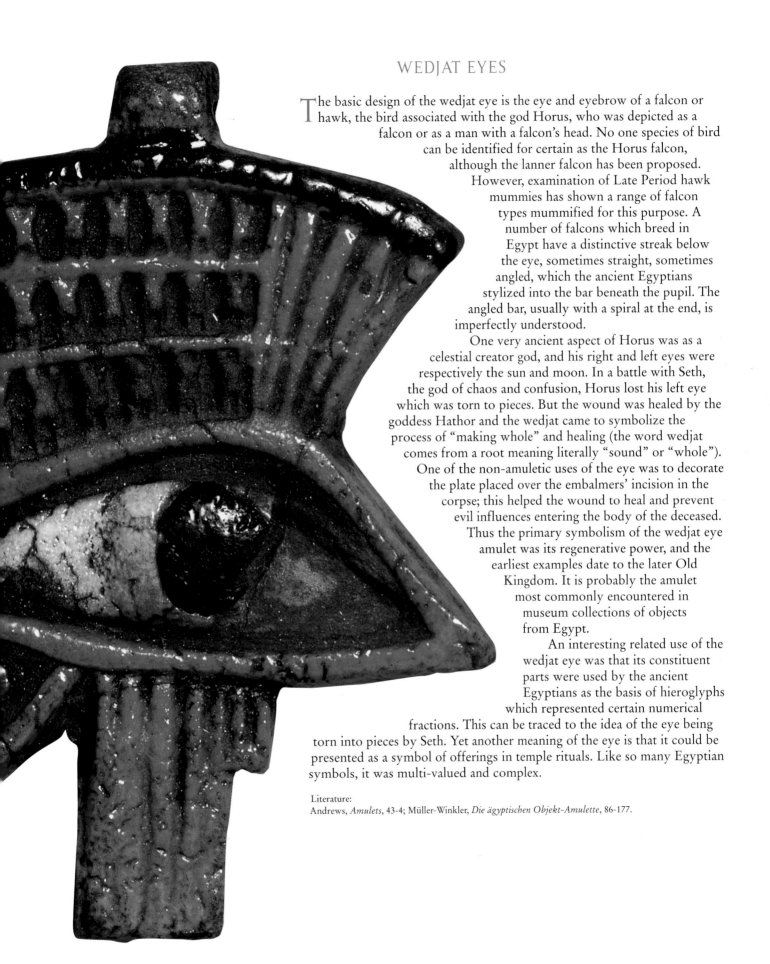

WEDJAT EYES

The basic design of the wedjat eye is the eye and eyebrow of a falcon or hawk, the bird associated with the god Horus, who was depicted as a falcon or as a man with a falcon's head. No one species of bird can be identified for certain as the Horus falcon, although the lanner falcon has been proposed. However, examination of Late Period hawk mummies has shown a range of falcon types mummified for this purpose. A number of falcons which breed in Egypt have a distinctive streak below the eye, sometimes straight, sometimes angled, which the ancient Egyptians stylized into the bar beneath the pupil. The angled bar, usually with a spiral at the end, is imperfectly understood.

One very ancient aspect of Horus was as a celestial creator god, and his right and left eyes were respectively the sun and moon. In a battle with Seth, the god of chaos and confusion, Horus lost his left eye which was torn to pieces. But the wound was healed by the goddess Hathor and the wedjat came to symbolize the process of "making whole" and healing (the word wedjat comes from a root meaning literally "sound" or "whole"). One of the non-amuletic uses of the eye was to decorate the plate placed over the embalmers' incision in the corpse; this helped the wound to heal and prevent evil influences entering the body of the deceased. Thus the primary symbolism of the wedjat eye amulet was its regenerative power, and the earliest examples date to the later Old Kingdom. It is probably the amulet most commonly encountered in museum collections of objects from Egypt.

An interesting related use of the wedjat eye was that its constituent parts were used by the ancient Egyptians as the basis of hieroglyphs which represented certain numerical fractions. This can be traced to the idea of the eye being torn into pieces by Seth. Yet another meaning of the eye is that it could be presented as a symbol of offerings in temple rituals. Like so many Egyptian symbols, it was multi-valued and complex.

Literature:
Andrews, *Amulets*, 43-4; Müller-Winkler, *Die ägyptischen Objekt-Amulette*, 86-177.

FIGURE OF ANUBIS

EA 61014

Faience

Provenance unknown

Late Period, 664-305 bc

Height 5.26 cm; Width 1.57 cm; Depth 2.23 cm

Acquired from the collection of Giovanni d'Athanasi in 1837

This amulet represents the jackal-headed god Anubis, standing, wearing a wig and a pleated kilt. It is pierced at the back to enable it to be suspended on a necklace.

FIGURINE OF ISIS AND HORUS

EA 63797

Faience

Provenance unknown

30th Dynasty or early Ptolemaic Period, 4th–3rd century bc

Height 12.2 cm; Width 3.13 cm; Depth 5.94 cm

Acquired in 1934

M any figurines showing Isis and Horus were made to be dedicated to one or both deities as votive offerings. A large number of examples in bronze are known, but specimens in faience such as this are less common. Here the workmanship is detailed and fine. The rich blue-green color of the glaze has been offset by a purplish coloring applied to the wig of Isis. The goddess wears on her head the image of a seat or throne (the hieroglyphic sign for her name). She clasps her right breast with one hand and with the other supports the head of her son to suckle him. Horus sits passively on his mother's knee; his head is shaven but for the curled sidelock of hair, denoting his youthfulness.

The mythology surrounding the god Horus was complex. It encompassed several originally distinct strands which were eventually woven together into a consecutive narrative. One element of the myth was that of the protection of the child Horus by his mother Isis when Seth sought to destroy him. So popular was this myth that Horus-the-Child (or Harpocrates) became an individual deity, distinct from other forms of Horus. He is often depicted in single figures or as part of a group showing him on the lap of his mother, who suckles him.

TRIAD OF ISIS, NEPHTHYS AND HORUS

EA 26317

Blue-glazed faience

Provenance unknown

Late Period, 664-305 bc

Height 4.11 cm; Width 3.20 cm

Acquired in 1895

A very popular amulet in the Late Period was a miniature sculptural group representing three important deities who played parts in the mythology of Osiris. In this example, Horus the child stands in the center, his youthfulness indicated by his nudity and the sidelock of hair worn on his head. He is flanked by his mother the goddess Isis and her sister Nephthys.

FIGURINE REPRESENTING A SOW AND PIGLETS

EA 64609

Faience

Provenance unknown

26th Dynasty, 664-525 bc

Height 3.53 cm; Width 0.87 cm; Length 5.50 cm

Acquired from the collection of M.W. Acworth in 1946

Literature: Andrews, *Amulets*, 35, fig. 32.

This small amulet is a vivid depiction of a sow with her young—creatures which must have been familiar to all Egyptians but which were not commonly depicted in art. Bristles stand up along its back and its curly tail is well rendered. Beneath its body, suckling at the teats, are seven piglets—four on one side, three on the other. A substantial ridged suspension loop is affixed to the top. Amulets such as this began to appear during the Third Intermediate Period. Some are inscribed with the name of Isis, others with that of Nut, and it is the character of this latter goddess which helps to explain the meaning behind these figurines.

The sky goddess Nut, who was also the mother of Osiris, was believed to give birth to the sun at dawn and to swallow it again at sunset. She also gave birth to the stars in the evening and swallowed them again in the morning. Decorated coffins and papyri contain many depictions of Nut's body forming the celestial canopy, arched above the earth, and studded with stars. The Egyptians also found a parallel for this notion in the more mundane sight of a mother-pig suckling her young. This image conveyed the maternal qualities of Nut, and no doubt the Egyptians were also intrigued by the sow's reputation for devouring her own piglets, just as Nut swallowed her children, the stars, only to bring them forth again. The amulet, therefore, could provide its wearer with fecundity and might also promote the endless repetition of the life-cycle, which the Egyptians so earnestly desired.

5

CULT OF THE
DEAD

The origins of the Egyptian cult surrounding death and burial can be traced back to the earliest prehistoric cultures, in particular those of Upper Egypt. By at least 4500 *bc* the Egyptians were providing the dead, laid usually in pits in the ground, with pottery to contain sustenance for their souls. By the later Predynastic Period (c. 3200 *bc*), social stratification was developing to levels which presaged the different social classes of the historic period. In keeping with this trend, tombs began to increase in size, particularly for the elite, and considerable numbers of vessels could be placed in a tomb. Thus the stage was set for the tomb developments of the great periods of Egyptian culture.

The tomb was always the major focus for the cult of the dead. Its early development probably paralleled the changes in social stratification just mentioned. The practice of mummification developed. Early elite tombs consisted of a chamber under a mound-like superstructure; the number of chambers around the central burial chamber increased in number, and this is most clearly seen in the burials of the kings of the 1st and 2nd Dynasties at Abydos (c. 3000-2800 *bc*). The cult of deceased kings was probably carried out in large enclosures which were physically separated from the places of burial, while it would seem that the non-royal cults were practiced in front of niches and small stelae on the exterior of the tomb. The development of this central mound led to the bench-shaped flat-topped tomb built of stone or mud-brick which Egyptologists term a *mastaba*. In the royal sphere, this led to the pyramid shape, and for private officials the mastaba remained throughout the Old Kingdom as the standard type of tomb. Here we are concentrating on the private persons; the niches and small stelae on the exterior were later superseded by offering chapels in the body of the mastaba, with the burial in a chamber at the bottom of a (usually deep) shaft.

Free-standing tombs of the mastaba type could only be built in areas where there were large flat spaces in which to establish a necropolis; such sites include Giza, Saqqara and Abydos. In many places along the river Nile the most suitable locations were in the cliffs on either side of the river, and so numerous chapels with shafts were cut into these rocks from the later Old Kingdom down to the New Kingdom. Some of the best known places where this type of tomb prevailed are Beni Hasan, Amarna and Thebes.

Tombs of all types, where the owner had suitable status and could afford to pay craftsmen, were decorated. This decoration was not random but was in various ways closely associated with the primary functions of the tomb, to act as a "machine" for ensuring the continued life after death of the deceased and for providing the provisioning, real or magical, necessary for the sustenance of the souls. Thus the most common scenes, in the Old Kingdom at least, show offerings of food, lists of offerings, the making of bread and beer and the preparation of meat. It is believed that the Egyptians thought these could all come into being by magic if real provision should fail. These scenes were supplemented by those of a more complex nature which probably are to be interpreted as symbolic ways of expressing hopes and wishes for rebirth after death. These scenes, in varying arrangements, continued to appear in tombs as long as they were decorated.

In general, the ancient Egyptians buried their dead in cemeteries not far from where they lived and worked. At certain periods, however, it became customary to commemorate oneself where possible at the important religious site of Abydos. In the Middle Kingdom, numerous small mud-brick chapels were set up near the cult centers of Osiris, the god of the dead, so that the deceased could partake in the mysteries of that god and make an additional expression of piety which he hoped would stand him in good stead in the next life. Several stelae in this exhibition come from such chapels, and are among hundreds of monuments from the site in all major world museums. Some officials were even fortunate enough to actually set up their final resting places in the Abydene cemeteries. The reader cannot fail to be struck by the variety of styles of these stelae, even though their basic purpose was the same. This practice of setting up stelae also continued in the New Kingdom, although the chapels themselves are no longer readily identifiable. In the latter period, stelae were more likely to be set up inside or outside the owner's actual tomb to form part of the decoration.

Other important elements of the tomb were statues and offering tables. The offering table included in this exhibition could be from a temple or a royal tomb, but it is of a design which was formulated in the Old Kingdom or even before. Offerings would be placed on these tables for the souls of the dead in the tomb, and they usually bore some carved representations of offerings for future eventualities. Tomb statues served various functions, the most important of which was to act as a place which the soul could occupy to receive offerings, and perhaps even take part in the tomb rituals. They also, through their inscriptions, helped to identify the tomb for both the spirits and the visitor—Egyptian statues rarely depicted anything but a generic human being, so the texts were necessary so that they became the person who paid for them.

Various rituals were performed at the tomb. Perhaps the most distinctive one took place at the time of burial. This was the "Opening of the Mouth," by which the eyes and mouth of the mummy were magically opened so that the deceased could see and breathe again. It is very likely that this ritual was also performed on statues and wall-scenes in the tomb so that they could come alive to fulfil their intended functions.

The most regular ceremony would have been the offering ritual, in which priests would come and offer food and drink before the offering places in the tomb each day. The core of this ritual is based around the formula "an offering which the king gives" (Egyptian *hetep-di-nesu*), which appears on almost every funerary monument. While it rapidly became a stock formula for the expression of the wish to receive offerings and benefits, the idea embodied in it is a wish that the king made offerings on behalf of mankind to certain named gods (most commonly Osiris and Anubis, but others are also found), who would then grant those offerings and other benefits to the dead. It is, in essence, a reflection of the ideal situation where all offerings are granted at royal and divine behest. The formula has a vast number of variants. As a basic simple example, one of the formulas on the border of the stela of Djehuty in this exhibit reads: "An offering which the king gives to Anubis, lord of the sacred land, that he may give invocation offerings of bread, beer, oxen, fowl, alabaster vessels, items of clothing, incense, *merhet* oil and all perfect and pure things on which a god lives to the *ka* of the overseer of the bureau Djehuty."

After samples of food were offered to the deceased, the remainder of the food which had been provided reverted to the priests or tomb endowment as payment for these services. Other rituals include the rites of transfiguration, whereby a priest would recite from a book of spells those texts which transformed the dead into eternal beings or *akh* spirits. The priests who carried out these rituals were usually lector priests or *sem* priests, ideally the eldest son of the dead, but one suspects that most often they were a group of professional men who made their living out of performing priestly service for several cults.

It has been indicated that magic permitted the Egyptians to believe that depictions of offerings could serve as well as the real thing. Thus, model offerings and model vessels were satisfactory, and in fact more durable substitutes for the originals. Offering lists written in hieroglyphs likewise provided enduring and very complete sustenance for the dead. These lists and depictions also included various sacred oils used for anointing the body, and which were deemed to be needed after death. In addition, these oils could be present in the tomb in jars or even, in the Old Kingdom, in the form of small slabs bearing their names, sometimes with a small depression for a sample of the oil.

Tombs were frequently reused, either by further members of the same family, or by usurpers unrelated to the original occupants. In the Third Intermediate Period in Thebes it was quite normal to sink a shaft into an older tomb, or even to clear out an existing shaft for one's burial. At that time the underground burial became the center of the further life of the deceased, with little or no formal offering place in an accessible area for the cult to be carried out. Considerable efforts were lavished on coffins, stelae and funerary figures, examples of which appear in various places in this catalogue. By the later Graeco-Roman Period, the wrapped mummy was normally the only item which went to the grave.

Literature:
Taylor, *Death and the Afterlife*
Grajetzki, *Burial Customs in Ancient Egypt*

Egyptian offering tables are of two main forms, those comprising a table on a stand, and those which consist of a large flat slab laid more or less directly on the ground. This large rectangular object is of the latter category. In the center of the slab are representations of the sorts of foodstuffs which might be expected to be offered; here we see two symmetrical ranges of jars, loaves, cakes and fowl framed on either side by tall libation jars and placed on a reed mat. Of more importance than illustrating what might be offered on the slab, these representations were believed to have the capability to come into being magically and to provide offerings for the recipient even if real items failed to materialize. Around the outside of the food representations is a line of hieroglyphs running clockwise around the table, with a prayer for offerings of a variety of items in the classic Egyptian measure of a thousand of each. Further from the viewer is a stylized loaf on the table, which gives the object the shape of the hieroglyph *hetep* "offerings;" through the middle of this loaf runs a small channel which was probably to allow water poured as libations over the offerings to run away.

The name of the king for whom this was set up has been erased, but it is evidently Amasis (Greek form; sometimes called "Ahmose II") the fifth king of the 26th Dynasty. Amasis is best-known for deposing his predecessor Apries and assuming the throne in about 570 *bc*. The cause of this revolt by the Egyptians was that Apries was thought to be giving too much preference to the Greeks and Carians who were becoming increasingly numerous in Egypt. The residence of the 26th Dynasty was at Sais where this table is supposed to have been found. The tombs of the kings are also reputed to have been at Sais (Herodotus II, 169) but have never been discovered. It is possible that this slab was intended either for an offering or even tomb-chapel of the king, or that it was placed in the main temple at the site dedicated to the goddess Neith.

The reason for the erasure of the name is uncertain. Either a later king was planning to reuse the slab, or else (perhaps) a disgruntled descendant of Apries might have damaged it in retribution for Amasis' coup.

OFFERING TABLE OF AMASIS

EA 94

Granodiorite

Said to be from Sa el-Hagar (ancient Sais)

26th Dynasty

Height 20.00 cm; Width 83.00 cm; Depth 73.00 cm

Acquired as part of the Salt Collection in 1823

Unpublished. See Wilson, *Egyptian Archaeology* 18 (2001), 3-5 for some
notes on recent excavations at the site.

57354

This is a typical example of a seated male figure of the later part of the Middle Kingdom. The man sits with both arms extended on his lap. He wears a long robe tied above his waist, which is a typical type of dress for an official of his day; the knot with which it is tied is clearly visible. He wears a smooth shoulder length hairstyle or wig with pointed lappets, which was popular in the 13th Dynasty.

The proper left-hand side of the statue is uninscribed, while the proper right bears an offering formula to Osiris. The texts on the statue are very worn and difficult to read. There are two further texts on the front and base of the seat, either side of the figure, also offering formulas, one to Osiris, lord of Ankhtawy (Memphis) and the other to Ptah-Sokar; it is quite likely that these are to be understood as formulas to the same necropolis deity, the composite Ptah-Sokar-Osiris. The name of the owner is not clearly preserved, but appears to be Iwy or Iay; the name of his mother is uncertain. His title appears to be that of "bowman."

This statue almost certainly was placed in a tomb or a commemorative chapel. Most Middle Kingdom statues in museum collections do not have precise provenances, although a few have excavated tomb contexts. For example, a statue of Tety, now in Pittsburgh, came from one of the northern cemeteries at Abydos, and an important discovery with better context was made in Luxor in 1999, when fragments of three such statues were discovered in the remains of some Middle Kingdom tombs close to the Ramesseum, the mortuary temple of Ramesses II. They, like the statue of Tety, were discovered in a simple shaft tomb, but were most likely set up in a small offering chapel near the mouth of the shaft, such as one of mud brick found by the excavators.

STATUE OF AN OFFICIAL

EA 57354

Granodiorite

Middle 13th Dynasty

Height 38.00 cm; Width 11.00 cm; Depth 20.00 cm

Acquired in 1924

Unpublished. Compare Porter and Moss, VIII, 378. See Patch, *Reflections of Greatness*, 30 for the Pittsburgh statue, and Nelson and Kalos, *Memnonia* 11 (2000), 131-51 for the tombs at Thebes mentioned above.

HEAD OF A WOMAN

EA 2381

Yellow limestone

Provenance unknown

18th Dynasty

Length 8.21 cm; Width 7.87 cm; Depth 5.30 cm

Acquired from the collection of Joseph Sams in 1834

Unpublished. Examples of private statues with similar hairstyles are
Hannover 1935.200.106 and Berlin 10675, both illustrated in *Ägyptens
Aufstieg zur Weltmacht*, 110-11. A well-known example, now shown not
to be authentic, is the statue of Tetisheri in the British Museum (EA
22558, Davies, *A Royal Statue Reattributed*). See Haynes, *JSSEA* 8
(1977-78), 18-24 for some notes on hairstyles in the 18th Dynasty.

This head would almost certainly have belonged to a seated statuette, to judge from parallels noted above. It is most likely that it was intended for a cult statue in a tomb, to be placed in a small niche somewhere inside the tomb chapel.

Little has survived from the statue to tell us anything about the woman depicted, as the missing lower parts of the figure would have borne her name. The most distinctive features are her broad face and the detailed heavy hairstyle or wig she wears. The long side locks of the hairstyle would originally have converged slightly towards the base of the neck, ending just above the breasts; the shoulders would have been largely bare. As part of the hairstyle hangs down the back of the head, it is known as the "tripartite" style, and—with variations—was the most common way of arranging women's hair from the 3rd Dynasty onwards. Distinctive features of this particular example are the evidence of a central parting, and the division of the locks into individual long tresses of hair, marked with a series of striations. This particular variant of the style is characteristic of the early 18th Dynasty, and is seen in various forms on coffins and statues. The broad smile of the face is also typical of the period.

In the course of the 18th Dynasty, the first major new female hairstyle for many years was introduced, in which the hair was arranged in one large mass which completely covered the shoulders and the upper back of the wearer. This style is known as the "enveloping" hairstyle and was the favored form for the remainder of the New Kingdom (see this section, object EA 460). The transition between the two styles seems to have begun about the reign of Thutmose III, and was certainly complete by that of Amenhotep III. Thereafter the tripartite style was reserved almost exclusively for depictions of goddesses.

UPPER PART OF THE STATUE OF A MAN

EA 124

Probably from Thebes

Mid 18th Dynasty

Height 58.00 cm; Width 36.00 cm; Depth 30.00 cm

Acquired as part of the Sams Collection in 1834

Unpublished. Compare Porter and Moss, I, 2nd ed. 790

The name of the owner of this statue is regrettably not preserved, as only the very beginning of an inscription has survived. This text would in full have expressed a wish for offerings to be left for the owner, perhaps in a temple. It shows a man seated with (originally) both his hands placed on his lap. The style of the statue with its long simple wig, short formal beard, and faint confident smile is typical of the middle of the 18th Dynasty, perhaps of the reign of Thutmose III or thereabouts. Note the so-called "negative space" between the upper arms and the body, as the arms and legs of Egyptian statues in stone are rarely separated from the main block which forms the body of the object. Although statues such as this were usually brightly painted, there are no traces of color surviving.

Statues such as this can come from either tomb or temple contexts, and it is rarely possible to decide between these two possibilities in the absence of detailed information about provenance. Private statues in hard stone are perhaps more likely to come from temples and those in limestone from tombs, but there are exceptions in both cases. The inscription on this statue is perhaps more suited to a funerary context. If that is so, the statue was probably placed in the offering chapel where it, and thereby the owner, could participate in the rituals which took place there.

Mahu and his wife Duat sit on a cube-shaped seat with a raised back. They both wear formal robes and wigs typical of the period in which they lived. His wig is long with elaborate lappets, while hers is a wig of the large enveloping type, with a particularly massive appearance. She wears a long robe, while he wears the typical outfit of an important official with a heavy front over the legs and large sleeves. Their skin is painted the conventional dark red-brown for men and yellow for women, while the wigs are black; most of the white paint which would have covered their robes has disappeared.

Offering formulas appear round the base, on the sides of the seats, and on the rear of the statues, which latter area is built up from above the seat back to give support to the statues and also to provide an enlarged area for texts. Further formulas are inscribed around the base and on the laps and legs of the figures. It is interesting that Mahu is mentioned both on his statue and also that of his wife, while she is only mentioned on her side of the sculpture. The quality of work of the statue is not of the highest, and the figures have a slightly disproportionately squat appearance, suggesting that the sculptor, while capable of producing an attractive statue, was not among the best in his profession. Mahu's title was "overseer of works of Amun in Thebes in Karnak," with the "in Thebes/Karnak" omitted in the text on his lap to save space.

This pair of statues was originally made to fit together, assuming that the recess for a joining block between them is ancient; certainly the chisel marks on the inner side of each statue do not accord with the original having been cut into two. There can be little doubt that statues of this type were made for installation into a tomb. The height of the figures is sufficiently restricted for them to have fitted into one of the niches which are prominent in tombs at Thebes, although no tombs inscribed for a Mahu with similar titles are known.

STATUES OF MAHU AND DUAT

EA 460

Probably from Thebes

19th Dynasty

Height 63.00 cm; Width 34.00 cm; Depth 27.00 cm

Acquired from the collection of Anastasi in 1839

Literature: Bierbrier, *Hieroglyphic Texts*, British Museum, Part 12 (1993), 25, Plates 92-95; compare Porter and Moss, I 2nd ed. 790.

STELA OF SA-ASET

EA 561

Limestone

Probably from Abydos

Mid-late 12th Dynasty

Height 63.00 cm; Width 41.00 cm

Acquired from the Anastasi Collection in 1839

Literature: *Hieroglyphic Texts*, British Museum, 2: Plate 25; *Des Dieux, des tombeaux, un savant. En Egypte sur les pas de Mariette Pacha* (Boulogne catalogue 2004), 189. Simpson, *Terrace of the Great God*, 20, pl. 60. See Franke, *Personendaten*, 311 (511).

The round-topped limestone stela of Sa-aset is divided into three registers. At the top are four lines of a hieroglyphic offering formula. These record the expression of the wish that Khentimentiu, lord of Abydos, will make offerings for Sa-aset. Khentimentiu, "foremost of the westerners," was an ancient god of the dead of the Abydos regions, many of whose attributes were assimilated by Osiris when his cult became centered at that site; thus, "foremost of the westerners" became one of the epithets frequently applied to Osiris from the Old Kingdom onwards.

The second scene shows Sa-aset standing at the left with a table of offerings before him and a libation basin below the table. To the right stand his father Za-meres and mother Isenperes, with a small figure of his sister Meret-Aset-Hathor between them. The scene is to be understood as the owner of the stela making offerings and libations to his parents.

The lowest scene contains six figures facing right. The first appears not to be named, but the others are two brothers and three sisters. No specific indication of the existence of a wife of Sa-aset is given on this stela.

On this stela, Sa-aset is given the titles "overseer of the land of Upper and Lower Egypt, overseer of the audience chamber." Although the provenance of this stela is formally unknown, from the prayers on it and the fact that its collector, Anastasi, worked at Abydos, it is reasonably sure that it originated in a chapel at that site. Other objects from the chapel of Sa-aset are a stela in Leiden (V 71) and an offering table in Cairo (CG 23006). His tomb was discovered at Dahshur in 1894, and the inscriptions there show that he obtained higher rank after his chapel at Abydos was completed, eventually holding the highest office in the land, that of vizier.

This round-topped stela has two main parts. The semi-circular area at the top ("lunette") is unusually filled with a series of vertical lines. The first main part consists of four lines of hieroglyphs. These take the form of a long offering formula to Osiris, here called "lord of Busiris," "foremost of the westerners," and "lord of Abydos." The invocation is on behalf of a man named Ameny, who was a "supervisor of the chamber of the Great House."

The lower part of the stela shows a large figure of the owner, behind whom are two sub-registers containing smaller depictions of members of his family. The upper row shows his mother Zatsekhmet and his father Zahathor and seemingly two women called "his sister Iyi." Below are four of his brothers, one shown smaller than the rest. A female figure "his sister Zatkhentykhetyt" straddles both registers. It is not abnormal for there to be no mention of a wife on the stela.

This is one of many stelae in the collection of the British Museum which came from the material assembled by the Armenian merchant and Swedish consul in Egypt, Giovanni Anastasi, in the 1820s and 1830s. These were sold at various times; Anastasi collected a great number of stelae from Abydos, which, together with the mentions of Osiris in the formula, make that site the most likely provenance for this specimen. This stela has thus far not been assigned to a particular offering chapel, although objects in Paris, Durham and Cairo may belong to the same man.

STELA OF AMENY

EA 565

Limestone

Probably from Abydos

Early to middle 12th Dynasty

Height 91.00 cm; Width 62.00 cm

Acquired from the Anastasi collection in 1839

Literature: *Hieroglyphic Texts,* British Museum, 2, pl 10. See Franke, *Personendaten,* 98 (106).

The stela of Dedusobek consists of two parts. In the upper area are eleven columns of hieroglyphs, which contain a series of laudatory epithets of the owner of the stela. Below, Dedusobek is seated at the left in front of an offering-table piled high with bread, meat and vegetables. To the right of the table stands his wife, named Hemet. Over the food are a number of hieroglyphs; those in the center refer to offerings in a thousand portions each of the commonest commodities in these formulaic descriptions: bread, beer, oxen, fowl, alabaster vessels and measures of cloth.

Dedusobek's principal title was as overseer of the *shenet*. This official seems in the Middle Kingdom to have been something of a policeman, perhaps even an inspector of police, and his other stela in the British Museum (EA 830) makes it clear that he was also a senior justice official at the Middle Kingdom capital of Itj-tawy, near modern Lisht. Although the specific find-spot of this stela is unknown, from associations with other monuments of Dedusobek, including another stela in the British Museum, one in the Louvre in Paris (C 240), and an offering table in Cairo (CG 23055) he must have had a chapel in Abydos like many of his contemporaries. It is probable that these objects were all made in the north and then later transported south to be set up in this chapel.

STELA OF DEDUSOBEK

EA 566

Limestone

Probably from Abydos

Middle 12th Dynasty

Height 100.50 cm; Width 61.00 cm

Acquired from the collection of Anastasi in 1839

Literature: *Hieroglyphic Texts,* British Museum, 4, pl 37; *Des Dieux, des tombeaux, un savant. En Egypte ur les pas de Mariette Pacha* (Boulogne catalogue 2004), 190; Simpson, *Terrace of the Great God,* 17, pl. 8. See Franke, *Personendaten,* 440 (763), and for his title, Helck, *Verwaltung,* 73-6.

566

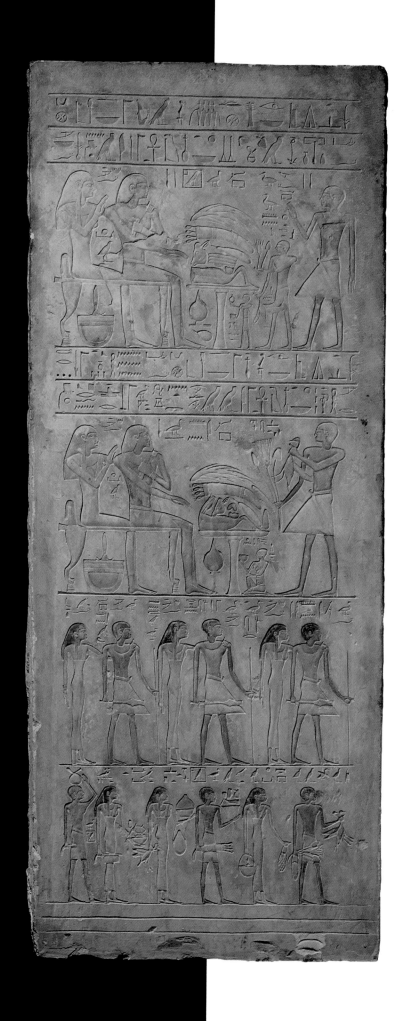

STELA (POSSIBLY) OF KHU

EA 571

Limestone

Probably from Abydos

12th Dynasty

Height 125.00 cm; Width 51.00 cm; Thickness 18.00 cm

Acquired from the collection of Anastasi in 1839

Literature: *Hieroglyphic Texts,* British Museum, 2, pl. 16. Detail of one scene, Parkinson, *Cracking Codes,* 169 (fig 54).

Stelae of the Middle and New Kingdoms are frequently filled with representations of the family and associates of the owner. This rectangular stela is of particular interest as it belonged either to a woman who married twice, or to two separate couples. The decoration consists of four scenes.

The upper two scenes both consist of an offering prayer to Osiris or Khentimentiu ("foremost of the westerners") with an offering scene below. The first of these scenes shows a couple, the steward Zahathor and his wife Khu receiving offerings from a son, also a steward, named Zamenkhet. The lower of the pair of scenes shows another couple, the steward Zaamun and his wife Khu, offered to by a servant named Sehetepu. The inverted mirror under the chair of the couples should be noted. Mirrors depicted in a funerary context, as here, are thought to signify new life, since their reflection of beauty could be associated with fertility and procreation.

The third register shows three couples; in each case the woman has her arm around the man. They are a son named Ameny with his wife Zatwoser, a son and priest named Senwosret with his wife Zatmontju, and another son, the steward Amenemhat and his mother Bet. The final scene shows six figures of both sexes carrying various foodstuffs and other offerings for the persons shown on the stela; their titles include servant, serving man, and butcher. Presumably they are dependants of the major personages.

The ownership of this stela and the family relationships are difficult to decipher. The female name Khu is common to both of the seated couples, but is this a case of a woman who married twice, or are they two (un)related couples, the wives in which happen to have the same name? Similarly, it is not clear whose are the sons mentioned in the third scene, as they are all referred to as "his son." We may tentatively suggest that the better scenario is that the stela was part of a chapel of the family of Khu, and that she remarried after her first husband died. Who that husband was is unclear.

STELA OF DJEHUTY

EA 805

Limestone

From Abydos

Later 12th Dynasty

Height 59.00 cm; Width 42.00 cm

Acquired in 1850

Literature: *Hieroglyphic Texts* Part 3, pl. 40; see Franke, *Personendaten,* 449 (779).

Like almost all stelae from Egypt, this example has several separate but complementary parts. Around the edge of the object runs a raised border on which is inscribed two offering formulas. Both begin facing each other at the top with the words "An offering which the king gives," and are very similar (but not identical) in content. Note how the writing of the hieroglyphs subtly handles the change in orientation from the rounded top ("lunette") into the vertical side: in both cases it happens with the beginning of the second part of the offering formula. The Egyptian offering formula basically has two parts, the naming of the king and the gods who will give what is requested, and then the offerings or other wishes themselves; in this case the second part begins with the expression of a wish for "invocation offerings."

The upper area of the interior of the stela bears nine lines of hieroglyphs. It begins with a brief formula requesting a perfect lifespan and justification (after death) for the owner, Djehuty, and then moves on to the formula known to Egyptologists as the "address to the living," in which visitors to the monument are encouraged to say a prayer for offerings for the owner if they wish various things to happen. In the case of Djehuty's formula, the wishes for which the visitor might pray include the following: that the temple of Khentimentiu (a form of Osiris, local to Abydos) might exist forever, and that the (visitor's) children might take their rightful places, in other words the position of their parents.

Two registers of scenes occupy the remainder of the stela. In the upper one, a male figure, doubtless the owner, is seated before a mass of offerings, including meat, vegetables, bread and jars of sacred oils. There are no texts, the inscription above providing the explanation. The lower scene is composed seemingly of Djehuty's relatives. At left, are a couple seated at an offering table; both persons bear the name Djehutyhotep, and are probably the parents of Djehuty; the father is called the offspring of Iti. At the right are three figures: a woman Tet, offspring of Djehutyhotep; Senebimy, offspring of Sathor, and "his beloved son" the serving man, Nubkau.

The mention of the temple of Khentimentiu makes it reasonably certain that this object comes from Abydos. It is in all probability from a chapel of the owner, although only one other monument has been associated with Djehuty, a stela in Cairo (CG 20065). That stela is thought to date to the reign of Amenemhat III, but this stela is somewhat later. Djehuty's main title was "overseer of the bureau," a reference to a department of the administration of the royal palace which was concerned with provisions. He was thus a middle-ranking official, and obviously important and wealthy enough to set up monuments at Abydos.

This large round-topped stela probably came from a tomb-chapel owned by Djehutymose. Its location is not known but it was probably in a New Kingdom necropolis in the area of Memphis. Djehutymose held the title of "chief of the keepers of the gate in Memphis," and so was presumably a senior security figure in the Egyptian capital city.

There is a scene within the round top ("lunette") of the stela, and a text in seventeen lines of hieroglyphs, with a sub-scene in the bottom left hand corner. The main image shows Djehutymose and his wife Khayet, together with his brother Nakht, in adoration before Osiris and Isis. The mummiform figure of Osiris is seated on his usual cube-throne, wearing the *atef* crown on his head and holding the crook and flail, symbols of kingship, in his hand. Isis stands with her arms protectively held to her spouse. Djehutymose is clothed in a short tunic and kilt, with a longer robe over it; the distinction between the outer and inner clothes is made by a careful mixture of sunk and raised relief work. Khayet wears a long flowing robe; similar variations in the technique of the relief carving are used to distinguish between the lines of her body and the outline of the robe. Nakht wears a short kilt and carries five ducks in his left hand.

The text is essentially an extended offering formula, but instead of concentrating on material offerings for Djehutymose, it expresses wishes concerning where he might go and what he might do in the afterlife, either in association with certain gods, or on certain days of the year.

The sub-scene shows a son pouring a libation to his seated parents. The son is called Nakht, and his parents' names are Tjay and Mesha. Nakht is wearing a carefully represented leopard skin which identifies him as a priest, either a *sem* or lector priest, although he is also playing the all important role of the "elder son" in attending to the cult of his parents. No further indication is given as to the relationship between these people and those at the top of the stela.

The stela can be dated to the later 18th Dynasty by the style of the robes and the elaborate wigs, which first come into use about the reign of Amenhotep III or a little before. Note also the difference in style between the hair and dresses of the women and that of Isis. Goddesses are shown in tight dresses with straps and tripartite wigs, which was also a normal style for private women until the mid 18th Dynasty.

STELA OF DJEHUTYMOSE

EA 155

Probably from Memphis

Later 18th Dynasty

Height 121.00 cm; Width 27.00 cm

Acquired from the collection of d'Athanasi in 1837

Literature: *Hieroglyphic Texts,* British Museum, Part 8: 47-9, pl. XXXIX. See Porter and Moss, III 2nd ed. 742

Neferabu was a workman who lived in the village of Deir el-Medina at Thebes, the community of craftsmen who worked on the royal tombs in the Valley of the Kings. This stela probably came from his tomb which was situated on the slopes surrounding the village, just above the site of the village shrines, where the Ptolemaic temple is also located.

The decoration on the stela is divided into three parts. At the top is a scene of the Opening of the Mouth ritual. Four mummies stand at the left of the scene; they are those of Neferabu, his wife Taiset, his mother Mahy, and probably his father Neferrenpet. Around them are two male and two female mourners, and in front are four persons. The first of these, a grandson, holds up the adze performing the ritual on the mummies, while the scribe Maanakhtef reads from a papyrus, followed by two women.

In the second scene, the jackal-headed god Anubis (or perhaps a priest with a jackal mask) leans forward over the mummy. This is a way of representing the embalmment of the deceased, and the jackal-figure is attended on by three sons, a grandson and two women. Genealogies of the family suggest that the mummy shown here is that of Neferrenpet, Neferabu's father.

The lowest part of the stela consists of eleven columns of hieroglyphs, beginning the "spell for proceeding to the tribunal on the day of burial" for Neferrenpet. The remainder of the text forms part of spell 1 of the *Book of the Dead*. The entire program of decorating the stela is to deal with the magical regeneration of the dead, which is why it most likely originated in the tomb.

The family of Neferabu and Neferrenpet is well known, not just from the tomb but from a variety of stelae set up by them. In addition to this and at least one other stela which surely came from the tomb, Neferabu set up some smaller votive stelae at shrines in or around Deir el-Medina. His tomb was probably originally discovered in the early years of the 19th century, at which time objects from it began to appear in various private and museum collections. The British Museum has two further stelae and part of the coffin of Neferabu; an ostracon in the museum can also be used to date Neferabu to the reign of Ramesses II.

STELA OF NEFERABU

EA 305

Limestone

Probably from Theban Tomb 5 at Deir el-Medina

19th Dynasty, probably the reign of Ramesses II

Height 63.00 cm; Width 42.00 cm

Acquired at the sale of the third Salt Collection in 1835

Literature: *Hieroglyphic Texts*, British Museum, Part 9, 36-7, Plate XXXII; Kitchen, *Ramesside Inscriptions* III, 770; Porter and Moss I 2nd ed. 728. Tomb TT5: Porter and Moss, I 2nd ed. 12-14; Vandier, *Mémoires publiés par les membres de l'Institut français d'archéologie orientale*, 69.

This round-topped stela is divided into three sections. At the top is a large curved hieroglyph representing the sky, below which is a winged sun-disc from which hang a pair of uraeus serpents. The hieroglyphs identify this as a representation of "he of Behdet," a term for the (originally) sky god Horus; this decoration is extremely common in the semi-circular "lunette" at the top of stelae.

The second and third parts are divided into left and right sides, with a scene above and a text relating to that scene below. On the left, Besenmut stands in adoration of the god Atum, represented in his usual form of a man wearing the double crown of Upper and Lower Egypt. Besenmut is dressed in a long white robe and wears the leopard skin of the priest. The text below in six lines is in two parts. Most of the first three lines are taken up with the genealogy of Besenmut, indicating

that he was a priest of the god Montu, and son of Nespasefy, also a priest of Montu, and Irtyru. The remainder of the text is a short hymn to Atum "who sets in life and is received into the underworld," referring to this deity as the eldest of the three phases of the sun. According to Egyptian belief, when the sun was born (rose) it was Khepri or Re-Horakhty, when it was mature (midday) it was Re, and it was Atum when it died (set) in the evening.

The scene on the right shows Besenmut in a similar pose before Re-Horakhty. Again his genealogy is given, plus a hymn to this god "who comes forth from Nun (the primeval waters)." The idea of the stela as a representation of the world is here enhanced by stressing the importance of the solar cycle in the concept of the rebirth of the deceased.

In the Third Intermediate and Late Periods such stelae were usually placed in the burial chamber with the coffin and mummy, although relatively few are known to have actually been discovered *in situ*. Many of the families of the priests of Montu of the 25th and 26th Dynasties were buried in small concealed shaft tombs within and around the precinct of the 18th Dynasty temple of Hatshepsut at Deir el-Bahari, an area which had been sacred since at least the Middle Kingdom. Although these tombs have produced many fine burial groups, regrettably very little was systematically excavated and most of the contextual information has been lost. The first temple on the site was that of Mentuhotep II of the 11th Dynasty, the remains of which are still visible today; the association between the priests of Montu and this much earlier king who employed the name of their god in his personal name (Mentuhotep means "May Montu be satisfied"), plus the sacredness of the site, must surely explain the choice of this area as a burial ground.

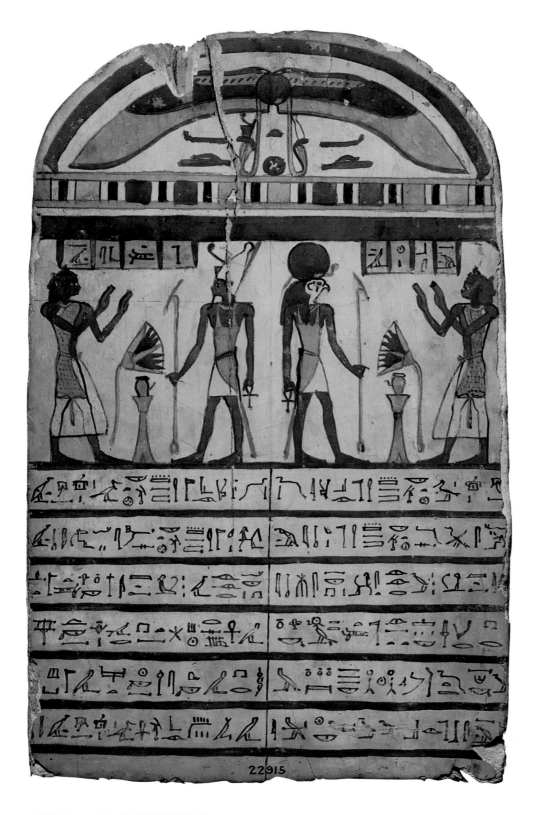

STELA OF BESENMUT

EA 22915

Sycamore fig wood, paint on plaster

Probably from one of the burials of the Priests of Montu at Deir el-Bahari in Thebes

Middle 26th Dynasty

Height 50.00 cm; Width 33.50 cm

Acquired from the Sabatier collection in 1891

Literature: *Hieroglyphic Texts,* British Museum, Part 11, 22, pl. 36-37; Compare Porter and Moss, I 2nd ed., 648. For a recent article on the burials of the priests of Montu see Sheikholeslami in Strudwick and Taylor (eds), *The Theban Necropolis,* 131-7.

PYRAMIDION OF HORNEFER

EA 479

From Deir el-Medina

19th Dynasty

Height 40.00 cm; Width 33.50 cm

Donated by Sir John Gardner Wilkinson in 1834

Literature: *Hieroglyphic Texts,* British Museum, Part 10: Plates 90-91; Rammant-Peeters, *Pyramidions Égyptiens,* 42-44 (39), Pl. XXIII-XXIV; *Art and Afterlife in Ancient Egypt,* No 24. The text is published in Kitchen, *Ramesside Inscriptions* III, 798. Compare Porter and Moss, I 2nd ed. 744.

Pyramids are perhaps the best-known symbol of Ancient Egypt. A pyramidion is a small mini-pyramid such as the present example. While readers tend to think of pyramids as the burial places of kings, pyramids were also at certain times employed as architectural features in the tombs of officials, notably in the second half of the New Kingdom and in the 25th and 26th Dynasties. Pyramids large and small were often capped by pyramidia.

At the apex of each of the four sides of this pyramidion is a small scene. One shows the sun-disc travelling in a boat, another shows Isis and Nephthys on either side of the symbol of the west with a falcon on top of it, while the third is damaged but probably showed the *djed* pillar of Osiris. The fourth shows a winged scarab pushing the solar disc along. In the larger areas of the four sides are depictions of Hornefer, his wife Nefertari, his son, also called Hornefer, his wife Webkhet, and another workman called Aahetepef. Pyramids were solar symbols, and it is thus not surprising to find on two sides of this object brief hymns of adoration to the rising and setting sun, accompanied by representations of Hornefer with his arms raised in the traditional Egyptian gesture of worship. In a band running above the vertical inscriptions Hornefer invokes various forms of the sun god.

Hornefer was a "servant in the place of truth," a title given to workmen who lived at Deir el-Medina and built the tombs in the Valley of the Kings at Thebes. The precise findspot of the pyramidion of Hornefer is not known, but from his title we can reasonably assume it came from Deir el-Medina, the community of the workmen and also their burial place. The site of his tomb is also unknown, although it was quite normal for tombs of workmen at Deir el-Medina to have small pyramids on top of their tombs. It is also possible that the pyramidion might have been deposited in a temple context as a votive object, as several examples of pyramidia come from temple locations at Deir el-Medina and Deir el-Bahari, where no tombs existed.

Stone vessels were common in burials from the Predynastic period and throughout the Old Kingdom—this was the greatest period of production of stone vessels in Egyptian history. However, in the course of the Old Kingdom there was a move away from larger "real" vessels to smaller model ones, and according to the principle of magical substitution, models of objects that were required for the spirits of the dead throughout eternity would be just as effective as the larger originals, while possessing the added advantages of being cheaper and easier to manufacture. These small vessels, known from at least the 3rd Dynasty, peaked numerically in the 4th-5th Dynasties, and then declined in popularity, as pottery became increasingly prevalent.

The character of these vessels as models should be immediately clear from the fact that the most difficult part of making any vessel other than a dish, the boring out of the interior, has only been minimally indicated in most cases. However, the exteriors of the vessels closely replicate larger examples, and although their finish varies somewhat, they are quite well made. In particular, the offering table, an essential central element to any offering display, is beautifully shaped and polished.

The ritual of offering for the dead was central to the function of the tomb. Real food would be left with the burial, but this of course could not be provided in sufficient quantities to supply the dead for ever. The mere existence of the model vessels, together with depictions of some of the offerings (even if just in hieroglyphs), was enough for the continued provision of sustenance to be assured.

This particular selection of vessels is part of a group of seventy-nine in the British Museum, found in the Sacred Animal Necropolis at North Saqqara in excavations of the Egypt Exploration Society. The baboon catacombs are part of a complex of animal cemeteries at North Saqqara; they are adjacent to the catacombs of the mothers of the Apis bull and very close to the falcon and ibis catacombs. These catacombs together with the major one, the Serapeum (burial place of the sacred Apis bulls) formed a major center of animal cults in the Late Period.

The animal cemeteries were constructed in an area which had previously been used for tombs of the Early Dynastic period and Old Kingdom. The earlier burials were actually made in Old Kingdom tombs on the desert escarpment, which later became incorporated into the larger catacomb galleries. Excavation notes indicate that these vessels were found adjacent to an Old Kingdom sarcophagus.

The boring marks are very evident in the jars and bowls, and there have not been any attempts to smooth them down. As indicated, the bores in the taller vessels are rarely more than 0.5 cm deep.

CIRCULAR MODEL OFFERING TABLE
EA 67257
Diameter 12.90 cm

MODEL DEEP BOWL
EA 67259
Height 2.50 cm; Diameter 4.10 cm

MODEL DEEP BOWL
EA 67261
Height 1.90 cm; Diameter 3.30 cm

MODEL DISH
EA 67263
Diameter 5.10 cm

MODEL DISH
EA 67273
Diameter 4.40 cm

MODEL DISH
EA 67278
Diameter 4.20 cm

MODEL SHALLOW BOWL
EA 67290
Diameter 3.80 cm

MODEL SHOULDERED JAR
EA 67326
Height 6.80 cm

MODEL CYLINDER JAR
EA 67327
Height 5.50 cm

MODEL SHOULDERED JAR
EA 67333
Height 5.50 cm

MODEL FLARED JAR
EA 67334
Height 6.20 cm
Of a type which is usually shown in tomb scenes as containing oils and sealed.

MODEL SHOULDERED JAR
EA 67335
Height 6.20 cm

A SET OF MODEL VESSELS AND OFFERING TABLE

All Egyptian alabaster (calcite)

From North Saqqara, baboon catacombs

5th Dynasty

Donated by the Egypt Exploration Society in 1971, from the excavations of Prof. Walter B. Emery; excavation number H5-1587

To be published in Sue Davies, *The sacred animal necropolis at North Saqqara. The mother of Apis and baboon catacombs. The archaeological report* (London, Egypt Exploration Society, forthcoming), section 5.3, object BCO-1398. The location in which these objects were found can be seen on the plan in *Journal of Egyptian Archaeology* 57 (1971), pl. II, lower plan, chambers near the west end. A similar set of jars from Giza is described in D'Auria, Lacovara and Roehrig, *Mummies and Magic*, 77-8.

MODELS OF EQUIPMENT FOR THE
OPENING OF THE MOUTH RITUAL

EA 58404

Tablet: limestone

Vessels: Egyptian alabaster (calcite) and limestone

Implements: schist and limestone

5th-6th Dynasties

Length 11.7 cm (tablet); Width 8.9 cm (tablet)

Length 1.9 cm (model vessels)

Length 3.5 cm (model implements)

Acquired in 1927

Literature: Taylor, *Death and the Afterlife*, 191 (fig. 134); discussed on pp. 164-5 and
190-2. See Roth, *Journal of Egyptian Archaeology* 78 (1992), 113-47 for discussion of
the role of the *peseshkef*. The Opening of the Mouth ritual is considered in detail in
Otto, *Mundöffnungsritual*.

The ritual known as the Opening of the Mouth was one of the most important acts performed before the mummy was placed in the tomb. Scenes on stelae, in tombs and on funerary papyri show the mummy standing upright outside the entrance to the tomb, with mourners and also priests performing parts of the ritual.

The aim of the ritual was to transform the mummy into a living and breathing being, at least in a magical sense. At the simplest level, it involved touching the mouth and the eyes of the mummy with a number of ritual implements, including adzes, magical fingers, and chisels, which would permit the mummy to breathe and see again, and permitted the *ka* spirit of the owner to move freely to and from the body. In its fullest representations, such as that in the 18th Dynasty tomb of the vizier Rekhmire at Thebes, it included nearly one hundred different stages, all illustrated in that tomb. Among the additional episodes which are more frequently depicted are scenes of slaughtering cattle and pouring libations.

The ritual probably originated as one performed on statues. It continued to be used on three-dimensional representations, and was also employed as part of the consecration of a temple: the eyes and mouth of each figure in a scene were magically opened so that they could fulfil all their intended functions.

This set of miniature models of real implements dates to the Old Kingdom. At that time it would appear that the ritual was different from and simpler than its later developed form: the objects here include small knife blades, some vessels, and in the center the strangely-shaped *peseshkef* implement, and not the mass of implements seen in later tomb scenes, which do include the *peseshkef*. The function of the latter implement has been debated. It may have supported the jaw of the mummy, or else might have played a part in the process of childbirth and thus have been used symbolically to bring about rebirth after death.

This small tablet is divided into seven sections by a series of vertical lines. At the bottom of each division is a lightly engraved column of hieroglyphs naming the seven sacred oils: *setji-heb, hekenu, seftji, nekhnem, twat, hatet-ash* (best pine/cedar oil), and *hatet-tjehenu*. Below each name is the hieroglyph of a sealed oil jar. Some slabs have small depressions beneath the names but this example does not.

These seven sacred oils were an important element in the Egyptian burial and offering rituals. Their names first occur on jar labels from the royal tombs of the 1st Dynasty at Abydos. Although the precise identification of the oils is not certain, there is little doubt that they were used for anointing the body at particular points in the funerary rituals. It was very important that they be present in the tomb to ensure the continuity of their ritual function, either in reality or by magic, and they appear in the Old Kingdom not only on tablets like this but also in relief around offering places and in actual lists of offerings.

Several similar oil tablets have been found in the course of excavations, and were always placed in burial chambers. The depressions in the surface (where they occur) were intended as repositories for small quantities of the oils, each associated with its name and ready for use. Jars containing larger quantities of the oils would perhaps also be placed with the funerary equipment, to be ready for use when needed.

TABLET WITH THE NAMES OF SEVEN SACRED OILS

EA 29421

Egyptian alabaster

Provenance unknown

Old Kingdom

Length 14.00 cm; Width 8.20 cm

Acquired in 1897

Unpublished. A similar example in Boston appears in D'Auria, Lacovara and Roehrig, *Mummies and Magic*, 81-2; an example in the British Museum in Taylor, *Death and the Afterlife*, 191 (fig. 134).

A "SOUL HOUSE"

EA 32612

Ceramic

Provenance unknown

Height 15.00 cm; Width 27.50 cm; Length 32.80 cm

Acquired in 1900

Unpublished. Compare Taylor, *Death and the afterlife*, 106-7. Many soul houses were found at Deir Rifa: see Petrie, *Gizeh and Rifeh*.

In ancient Egypt from the end of the Old Kingdom until the Middle Kingdom, the more wealthy tomb owners built chapels, the walls of which were decorated with scenes of offerings and other commodities needed for their afterlife. Wooden models of servants preparing food were also included among the burial goods. Less wealthy individuals had only shaft tombs and models. These were different ways of providing sustenance for the dead in the afterlife. Poorer individuals of the same period were normally buried in simple shafts with none of the expensive wall-scenes and objects. Instead they were often provided with a ceramic platter or model house which would provide them with a representative selection of offerings. These objects were often called "soul houses" by Egyptologists, as it was originally thought that they might be a representation of an abode for the *ka* spirit of the deceased, although this is now thought to be less likely, the representations of food offerings being more important. However, it is possible that these often crudely made models can be used to give some idea of what a typical dwelling might have looked like.

The present example is an oval platter on which is a small shelter or room with a curved roof at the rear. In front of this room are arranged a number of food items. These include some pots (which are to be understood as containing food), some loaves of bread, and a number of joints of meat, all highly relevant to the needs of the deceased. In the center at the front is a squarish offering table, with a small spout at the front which permitted libations to be poured (symbolically) over the offerings, and the water could then drain off. The latter feature can be seen on real offering tables (see this section, object EA 94).

6

FURNISHINGS OF THE
TOMB

Egyptian tombs tend to evoke images of the gold-filled chambers of Tutankhamun, and the question is often posed as to how representative this might have been of the contents of other tombs. It is of course quite likely that the tombs of other kings of the New Kingdom, such as Amenhotep III and Ramesses II, might have held comparable volumes of treasures, but what of the rest of the people of Egypt? Archaeology can provide a partial answer, although we are heavily dependant on the quirks of survival. It must be stressed that this section is chiefly concerned with objects buried with the body of the deceased in his burial chamber. Thus they were physically separate from the cult items discussed earlier in this catalogue which would have been in the area of the tomb set aside for ritual purposes.

The extent of tomb furnishing would depend on the social status of an individual, but the customs and fashions of funerary beliefs at the time were of equal importance. Some elements are reasonably consistent over time: pottery vessels for storing food for the deceased are an example, as they are ubiquitous from the Predynastic Period until after the New Kingdom, as is jewelry. But even pottery appears to be found less frequently in the 1st millennium *bc*; is this just because earlier archaeologists did not bother to record this material properly as it was thought to be unimportant, or did it become unfashionable to put such provisions in the burial chamber? Other changes were afoot at this time, for the Third Intermediate Period witnessed the reduction of burial equipment to coffins, shabtis, Osiris figures, stelae and the like, with virtually none of the "everyday life" items (including jewelry) which were common in earlier periods. The expense needed for some of these coffins indicates that these changes were not really due to economic circumstances, and the fact that each element in this restricted range of items had a well-defined function in ensuring the future life of the deceased suggests strongly that at some point funerary customs changed from what they had been before to a new simpler model, concentrating on what was deemed absolutely necessary.

These objects of the Third Intermediate Period are considered in other sections of this catalogue, so let us summarize practices from earlier times. In addition to pottery, Predynastic and Early Dynastic tombs frequently contained stone vessels and other stone items such as palettes, in quantities perhaps relative to the rank of the owner. Palettes, which may have been markers of status or have held an uncertain ritual function, cease to appear not long after the start of the 1st Dynasty, while stone vessels could occur in vast quantities in royal tombs. Nevertheless, their number also began to decline around the end of the 2nd Dynasty, although they remained in Old Kingdom burials right through to the 6th Dynasty, and are found occasionally thereafter. Headrests are particularly common from the Old Kingdom and Middle Kingdoms; these may have been used in life but are perhaps more likely to have been meant to ensure the integrity of the mummy and to offer support in the next world.

Wooden models were provided in increasing numbers during the First Intermediate Period and earlier Middle Kingdom. These may have been substitutes for scenes on the tomb-walls in some cases, notably in burials of mid-ranking officials, but they could also have acted as servants for the dead. Other than perhaps in quantity and quality, there are few overall differences in the equipping of elite tombs, although it must also be said that few such sepulchers have survived intact. Magical provision of many items was ensured by the so-called "object friezes" on many Middle Kingdom coffins. In this exhibition is one elaborate collar from a burial of a person privileged to be interred near the tomb of king Mentuhotep II; small and exquisite items of gold jewelry are also known from burials of people of varying status, in addition to the magnificent funerary jewelry of queens and princesses now in the Cairo Museum.

From the New Kingdom come the "classic" burials with many different types of objects. Again it must be stressed that most of what is known comes from a small number of intact burials of the elite official classes, overwhelmingly from the area of Thebes, and almost entirely of the 18th Dynasty. These burials include that of the foreman Kha from Deir el-Medina, now in Turin, and those of Maherpri and Yuya and Thuya in the Valley of the Kings, now in Cairo.

Many of the items from these tombs appear to be articles which might have been used in life, such as chairs and stools and decorative elements from them, cosmetic vessels, linen, games and musical instruments. It is indeed possible that the presence of such items in the burial was intended to ensure that they existed for the dead in the next life, but some have further potential meaning. Thus kohl containers for black eye paint might additionally provide material "back-up" for a spell in the *Book of the Dead* which relates to the deceased entering the presence of Osiris appropriately made-up. The types of luxury oils presumably placed in the glass or stone vessels could also provide divine fragrance for the dead. Much jewelry dates to the New Kingdom, and probably comes from mummies themselves or from boxes accompanying their owners in tombs. In addition to being merely decorative, some of the jewelry was amuletic in nature and could afford protection to its wearer; such pieces might have been worn in life before being buried with the owner.

After the later New Kingdom, as noted above, a reassessment of what was essential for a burial eliminated almost all of the luxury items which feature in this section of the exhibit. One exception to this is finger-rings, such as the massive ring of Sheshonq, which might have been buried with the high official and could even have been stolen from his mummy.

The reader will no doubt marvel at the amount of material buried by the Egyptians with their dead over more than three millennia. So much of what survives from Ancient Egypt comes from tombs that it is easy to forget that there were also objects of daily life. The difference is that while life was transitory, death/new life and its accoutrements were confidently expected to last much longer, and it was necessary to take the fullest precautions for survival. The prodigious quantities of burial goods in the British Museum and elsewhere show how well the Egyptians succeeded.

Literature:
Taylor, *Death and the Afterlife*
Grajetzki, *Burial Customs in Ancient Egypt*
Ikram and Dodson, *The Mummy in Ancient Egypt*

The squat folding stool is a piece of furniture known from tomb-paintings in Egypt from before the New Kingdom. This beautifully made example is of a type which appears to have been restricted to the 18th and 19th Dynasties, characterized by legs terminating in duck heads.

It is composed of three elements. The well cut and finished base rails are cylindrical and without further decoration. The folding legs are the most attractive part of the stool, for they each terminate in a head of a duck or goose. These heads are carefully carved, with the eyes and nostrils inlaid with ivory; there are also long thin triangular pieces of ivory inlaid into the neck of the bird. The third part is the seat rails. To these would have been attached a piece of leather to serve as the seat, and many traces of the leather remain on the underside of the rails. A particularly elaborate example of this type of stool was found in the tomb of Tutankhamun.

Whether the bird shown on the stool legs is a duck or a goose is unclear. Both, however, had symbolic meaning in addition to their purely decorative function. The duck was associated with eroticism and sexual reproduction, which of course are intimately connected with the symbolism of new life and rebirth - the purpose of the tomb. The goose is known as a symbol of the god Amun; ducks are generally more common as decorative motifs in wooden items than geese.

The poor preservation of domestic remains in Egypt, contrasted with the excellent potential for survival of funerary contexts, makes it certain that this stool was found in a tomb, one of the many discovered at Thebes in the hunt for antiquities to sell in the 1820s, when Henry Salt or one of his agents purchased it. The excellent quality of the piece means that it probably came from the tomb of an important and wealthy individual. It is not clear whether objects such as this were domestic items of the owner's, subsequently placed in his tomb, or were specially made for the burial. Whatever the case, the soul of the deceased was thought at the time to need furnishings in the afterlife.

WOODEN FOLDING STOOL

EA 2477

Wood inlaid with ivory, with leather seat

From Thebes

New Kingdom, probably 18th Dynasty

Height 53.30 cm; Width 54.60 cm

Acquired at the sale of the third Salt Collection in 1835

Unpublished. Compare similar examples in various museums in Killen, *Egyptian Furniture* I, 40-3, pl. 57-64.

GLASS VESSELS OF THE NEW KINGDOM

The ancient Egyptians did not produce glass on any scale before the New Kingdom, and it is in fact quite likely that earlier examples of glass came about as much by accident as by design. The technologies involved in the production of glass are not unrelated to those used with faience, and both materials (glass particularly so) were treated as artificial precious stones. Glass became a common luxury item for the elite from about 1500 *bc*; the technology required to produce glass is complex, and it is quite possible that access to it was controlled as a royal monopoly. One of the sub-periods in the 18th Dynasty during which considerable amounts of glass were made was in the reigns of Amenhotep III and Akhenaten, and possible production sites have been identified at Malqata in Thebes, at el-Amarna, and at Gurob. Although the basic materials needed for production—silica, soda and lime—were readily available, some of the colorants, for example cobalt, would have been sourced in Asia Minor or even further away.

It has been ascertained that the Egyptians could not have produced the temperature of around 1700°C needed to melt silica. Hence a flux would have been required; it is likely that the ingredients could have become sintered or fritted together (a state where the materials have reacted together but are not liquefied) at about 750°C. That material was probably allowed to cool and then ground up, at which point large unreactive particles could be removed. This powder might then have been heated to 1000-1200°C, at which point it was sticky and could be molded.

Glass vessels such as these were made around cores, probably of clay and dung, onto which the basic glass was applied, and then heated rods of colored glass were trailed over the body, while the core was rotated on a spindle. Combing of the still molten trails produced the beautiful threaded effect.

Vessels such as these were generally used to contain expensive cosmetics and oils. One example below is a container of a type specifically for eye paint. While it is quite possible that these were placed in the tomb as luxury items enjoyed during life, it would be typical of ancient Egyptian practice for them to have additional functions. The introduction to spell 125 of the *Book of the Dead,* the famous "negative confession," indicates that the deceased should go into the presence of Osiris "painted with black eye paint and anointed with myrrh." Perfume was also the aroma of the gods, and the whole purpose of the tomb was to ensure the transformation of the deceased into a semi-divine being for eternity.

Literature:
Nicholson and Shaw, *Ancient Egyptian Materials and Technologies*, 195-224;
Kozloff and Bryan, *Egypt's Dazzling Sun*, 373-82.

EA 47983

From Kahun

New Kingdom

Height 9.10 cm

Donated by W.M.F. Petrie in 1890 (originally in the collection of the Department of Greek and Roman Antiquities)

Literature: Cooney, *Glass*, 143 (1738). For the provenance, see Petrie, *Kahun, Gurob and Hawara*, 32.

This glass vase with a broken handle was found with a corpse simply wrapped in a bundle of reeds, and hence seems to be a rare example of a high-status object buried with a low-status owner. Other material from this burial suggested that it was made in the late 18th Dynasty.

The glass of the body and handles is opaque dark blue. On the neck is a chevron pattern in yellow and white, repeated in a slightly looser form on the body. A line of shallow indentations above the body decoration are probably the guide-points made when the body was viscous prior to the application of decoration.

Opposite Page

EA 4743

From Memphis

18th Dynasty

Height 10.00 cm

Purchased from the collection of James Burton in 1837

Literature: Cooney, *Glass*, 142 (1734), pl. VIII.

This jar has a cylindrical neck and a hollow trumpet-shaped base with a flat rim. It is made of dark-blue glass with decoration applied in pale yellow, pale blue and white. One of its original four handles has been lost.

GLASS VESSELS OF THE NEW KINGDOM

EA 22819

Provenance unknown

18th Dynasty, perhaps the reign of Amenhotep III or later

Height 9.30 cm

Literature: Cooney, *Glass*, 147 (1755), pl. VII; Kozloff and Bryan, *Egypt's Dazzling Sun*, 383-4.

The form of this superb vessel is based on that of the ceramic type known as a base-ring II jug. These were imported into Egypt during the late bronze age from Cyprus, and the shape is relatively rare in glass, perhaps in part because removal of the mold around which the vessel was made was difficult and may have left a great deal of residual core inside.

The body is of purple-blue glass with chevron decoration in light blue and yellow. The handle (now broken) was made from three or four separate sticks of glass to give a striped effect, while the foot and rim are made from added prefabricated blue and yellow sticks of glass. It has been suggested that this vessel has affinities in its manufacture with other glass vessels made at Gurob.

EA 64342

Provenance unknown

18th-19th Dynasties

Height 8.80 cm

Donated by Sir Augustus Wollaston Franks in 1889
(ex Rogers Collection)

Literature: Cooney, *Glass*, 143-4, pl. VI (1743).

An intact translucent grey-blue jar with two
handles. The vessel has a wide neck and a
separately-made rim. The body and neck are
decorated with a festoon pattern in trailed
light-blue glass.

EA 2589

Provenance unknown

18th Dynasty

Length 10.00 cm (tube); Length 11.20 cm (applicator)

Acquired at the sale of the third Salt Collection in 1835

Literature: Cooney, *Glass*, 147 (1756); Kozloff and Bryan, *Egypt's Dazzling Sun*, 388-9; *Art and Afterlife in Ancient Egypt,* No 40.

This attractive kohl-tube is made of dark-blue glass in the form of a
palm column. The elements of the palm capital at the top are indicated
with a white thread of glass, and there is a series of six horizontal bands
of pale blue glass below. On the lower part of the body are white and
blue chevrons. The core is still evident inside, colored red-brown. The
tube is accompanied by a glass applicator with a typical bulbous end.

Kohl is the name given to the black eye paint favored by the ancient
Egyptians. In the New Kingdom it was either stored in small squat jars
of stone or in attractive column-shaped vessels as with this example. The
tall shape accommodates well the associated applicator, and also permitted the Egyptians to reproduce a plant shape so associated with new life.
It has been observed that the proportions of this kohl tube reproduce
the proportions of the columns in the temple of Amenhotep III at Soleb
in Nubia, and that its manufacturing style might mean that it was made
at that king's palace at Malqata in Thebes.

JAR BEARING THE NAME OF PEPY I

EA 22559

Egyptian alabaster

Provenance unknown

6th Dynasty

Height 15.60 cm

Acquired in 1890

Unpublished. Compare related objects bearing royal names in *Egyptian art in the time of the Pyramids*, 448-55, and a vessel with similar a similar inscription in Berlin in Hölzl, *Die Pyramide Ägypten,* 220-1. See Quirke, *Who were the Pharaohs* for further information about different royal names.

This cylindrical jar with a wide rim and a flat foot is of a type which became common for a period in the 6th Dynasty; many vessels with similar inscriptions of Pepy I and Pepy II are known, but few mention other kings. These jars show the skill with which craftsmen of the later 3rd millennium *bc* could work stones such as alabaster. The white veined color of this stone was particularly attractive to the Egyptians, and was very popular in the Old Kingdom. Its relative softness meant that it could be worked more easily than the harder stones so favored in the Predynastic and Early Dynastic Periods.

This vessel bears inscriptions filled with blue pigment. The vertical hieroglyphs give the titulary of Pepy I. On the right is the main cartouche name of the king, his birth name Pepy, with the title "king of upper and lower Egypt," within the cartouche he is also called "son of Hathor mistress of Dendera." Numerous monuments of this king attest to his piety towards this particular deity. The middle name is his Horus name, Merytawy, written in a *serekh* (perhaps imitating the exterior of an early type of brick palace). The left-hand column gives two of his other names, the *nebty* or "two ladies" name, Merykhet, and the so-called "Golden Horus" name, which is not easy to translate but is written with three falcons. The only name missing from the jar is the second cartouche or throne name, *Meryre*. In one horizontal line at the bottom is repeated twice "given life and dominion forever."

These jars were perhaps luxury productions of royal workshops. Although none have been found in a good archaeological context, they may have been placed in the royal burial or given as marks of favor to important officials of the time.

VESSELS OF HARD STONE

Very early in their culture, the Egyptians were able to develop an astonishing ability to work hard stone into beautiful vessels, large and small, with only relatively simple tools. As with most working of hard stone in Egypt, the primary means of shaping and grinding was by using other very hard stones, accompanied by drills with stone or copper bore heads; stones which seem to have been used for boring include chert, diorite, flint and quartzite but even softer stones such as limestone and sandstone were employed. Marks inside vessels from the Naqada I Period (c. 4000 *bc* onwards) show that drills were in use even at that early date. Either the vessel was turned or the drill itself rotated to produce the vessel. A number of tombs of Old Kingdom date, and a few from later periods, contain wall scenes which show a variety of drills in use, in particular the crank drill, often accompanied by weights to improve performance. Further shaping and final polishing would have been achieved by rubbing with other stones. As we stand and marvel at the quality of these vessels, we must recall that each vessel in hard stone would have taken many hours to produce, and thus they must have been expensive luxury items for the elite, an expression of their wealth and importance.

The Predynastic and Early Dynastic Periods were the heyday of the production of vessels in stone, particularly hard stones; two such vessels are presented here. They were made in vast numbers in some periods; for example, in the warren of galleries beneath the Step Pyramid enclosure of Netjerikhet Djoser at Saqqara, it is estimated that one hundred thousand of such vessels were placed, dating to the 2nd Dynasty as well as the early 3rd. Stone vessels have been found in considerable numbers in Old Kingdom tombs, but most of these were made from softer stones such as Egyptian alabaster and limestone, which could presumably be manufactured more easily than those of hard stone.

Stone vessels continued to be made throughout Egyptian history, but nothing approaching the scale of the 4th and 3rd millennia *bc*. They remained luxury items, and appeared mostly in burials of royalty and high-status persons. From the little evidence that survives, it would appear that they were used above all for perfumes and valuable oils. The large serpentinite jar here fits into this category.

Vessels were made from a wide range of stones. Hard stone appears among the earliest examples; thus basalt vessels are prominent among the Naqada I material mentioned above. The study of Aston noted below should be consulted for detail on these stones, but they include marble and serpentinite as here, and quartz, Egyptian alabaster, steatite, granodiorite, granite, and limestone, to name but a few. Most of the harder stones were obtained from quarry sites at some distance from the main Egyptian Nile valley.

Literature:
Aston, *Ancient Egyptian Stone Vessels* introduces the materials and forms used in Egypt; see also Lucas and Harris, *Ancient Egyptian Materials and Industries*, 421-8 and Sparks, in *Cultural Interaction in the Ancient Near East*, 53-5, which summarizes much of what has been said about the process of manufacture. Modern experiments in the techniques can be found in Stocks, *Experiments in Egyptian Archaeology*, Chapter 5. Examples of such vessels will be found in the publications of all major museums.

EA 35075

Serpentinite

Provenance unknown

Predynastic

Height 7.90 cm; Diameter 11.50 cm

Acquired in 1901

Unpublished. See Aston, Harrell and Shaw in Nicholson and Shaw, *Ancient Egyptian Materials and Technologies*, 56-7 for some notes and further references to serpentinite.

A squat serpentinite jar with two tubular handles. Serpentinite is the more geologically correct name for the material usually called "serpentine." Several variants of this stone were available in Egypt, varying mostly between green and black in color. Many vessels were made of this stone in the later Predynastic Period, but it was also in use during the New Kingdom; at that time it was also commonly used for scarabs and other smaller objects.

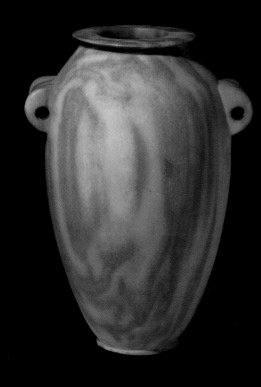

EA 35297

Marble

Provenance unknown

Early Dynastic Period

Height 34.20 cm; Diameter 9.40 cm; Diameter 14.20 cm

Acquired in 1901

Literature: Spencer, *Early Dynastic Objects*, 32, pl. 15 (156). See Aston, Harrell and Shaw in Nicholson and Shaw, *Ancient Egyptian Materials and Technologies*, 44-5 for some notes and further references on marble.

This superb tall shouldered vase is made of grey and white striated crystalline marble. It has a flat base and convex body with two horizontally pierced tubular handles and a broad flat-topped rim. The outer surface of the handles is concave, and the interior is well hollowed-out. It is clear that this vase was made with exceptional care, and is an excellent example of the level of craftsmanship the Egyptians were able to attain at this period.

Marble was not a stone which was used very often in Dynastic Egypt (although there does seem to be a small concentration of statues from it in the Hatshepsut and Thutmose III Period), and it is of course most closely associated with the Classical world. Very few vessels in this material have been identified, and it has been frequently confused in the past with highly colored limestones, particularly by specialists under the influence of classical stone carving. Sources of marble in Egypt are to be found in the hills of the Eastern Desert, between the Nile and the Red Sea.

EA 24432

Serpentinite

Provenance unknown

18th Dynasty

Height 31.80 cm

Acquired in 1891

Unpublished. For serpentinite see references above. Parallels for the shape are noted in Aston, *Ancient Egyptian Stone Vessels*, 151; some New Kingdom examples are in Lilyquist, *Egyptian Stone Vessels* and *The tomb of three foreign wives of Tuthmosis III*, 212.

This is a large, well-made jug with a handle and separate lid (broken and repaired). It has a narrow base and a well-formed rim. Below the rim, where the top of the handle joins the neck, are two horizontal bands which are an extension of the handle and were presumably intended as a decorative feature, although they might conceivably also replicate the appearance of a cord-based handle from an earlier era.

Elaborate stone vessels of this type in the New Kingdom come almost exclusively from very elite contexts; the examples in the references here to publications by Aston and Lilyquist come from the Valley of the Kings and other royal tombs. Such vessels were used to contain high-value and exclusive products, probably oils and perfumes.

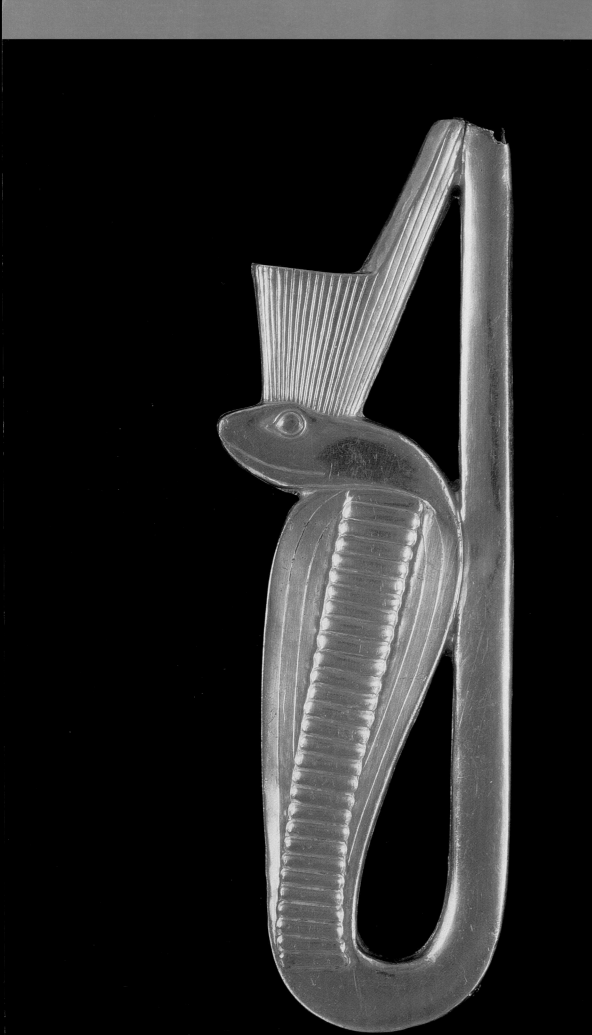

GOLD COBRA WEARING THE RED CROWN OF LOWER EGYPT

EA 16518

Sheet gold

Provenance unknown

Late Period, after 600 bc

Length 13.6 cm

Acquired in 1886

Literature: Quirke and Spencer, *The British Museum book of ancient Egypt*, 69, fig. 49; *Gold and Civilization*, Catalogue Australia 2001, 117.

The cobra was a much feared and respected creature in Egypt. It possessed many different associations, particularly with royalty, and use of the symbol meant that the dangerous power of the cobra was always magically turned to the benefit of the user. Thus the king's uraeus, worn on his brow, is referred to in some battle texts as destroying his enemies and giving the king power over them. Images of Egyptian gods also bear the rearing cobra. This cobra could be interpreted as either Hathor who, in the guise of the eye of Re, was sent to destroy mankind for being disrespectful, or as Sekhmet who was the fiery weapon of the god Re and who could also be sent out to destroy the enemies of the gods. Re bequeathed this gift of potential destruction, represented by the rearing cobra, to his descendants, the kings of Egypt.

The rearing cobra also represents the goddess Wadjet, patron of the town of Buto. She and the vulture goddess Nekhbet, of el-Kab, represented Lower and Upper Egypt respectively and were shown wearing the appropriate red and white crowns. Together they were the tutelary goddesses of the third name of the king, the so-called "two ladies" name, placing him under their protection. Hence the *uraeus* represents both Wadjet and the power immanent in the cobra.

The cobra was used as a decorative element on furniture, vessels and jewelry. The fact that the cobra from this decorative ornament wears the red crown of Lower Egypt means almost certainly that it represents Wadjet. The fine workmanship and the material used suggest that it belonged to a piece of elite, perhaps royal, furniture, such as a chair.

HEADREST

EA 30413

Yellow marble

Old Kingdom, c. 2300 bc

Height 21.5 cm; Width 17.0 cm; Depth 7.2 cm

Acquired in 1898

Literature: *Art and Afterlife in Ancient Egypt*, No 69.

The decoration of this headrest is quite austere, as was often the case with objects of Old Kingdom date. Its form is quite simple, with decorative fluting on the sides of the shaft. The surface of the stone has been smoothed, but not highly polished.

Egyptian headrests retained the same basic shape throughout their long history. Old Kingdom examples were frequently of stone, while later examples were of both stone and wood. There is some uncertainty as to whether headrests were used during life or were made specifically for the tomb. It has been argued that some examples show signs of wear, but almost all provenanced specimens come from tombs. It is more likely that wooden headrests could have been used in the home, but the elaborate nature of some examples, in particular those which bear the name of their owner, must surely mean that they were made for the tomb.

In the tomb, headrests were placed close to the head of the mummy, either on top of the coffin, or within it. The classic position for the mummy in the late First Intermediate Period and Middle Kingdoms was for it to be laid on its left side with the head supported by a headrest. This position might reflect the conception of death as sleep. There was also a notion, found in the Coffin Texts that the headrest would help to prevent the head being severed from the body.

Full-size headrests were most common as tomb equipment from the Old Kingdom down to the New Kingdom. They appear to have fallen out of fashion in the Third Intermediate Period, although an element of their function was re-evoked at the end of that period with the appearance of the headrest amulet (see Section 4, Trappings of the Mummy, Object EA 12001).

Above:

EA 25360

Wood

From Meir, Middle Egypt

12th Dynasty, around 1900 bc

Length 113.00 cm; Depth 12.10 cm

Acquired from Jacques de Morgan in 1894

Literature: Glanville and Faulkner, *Wooden model boats*, 16-19, plate IIIc (10). A note in *Annales du Service des Antiquités d'Egypte* 1 (1900), 65 indicates that de Morgan found boats at Meir in 1892-3. Stead, *Egyptian life*, 33-34, fig. 44; Quirke and Spencer, *The British Museum book of ancient Egypt*, 12-13, fig. 2.

This is a wooden model of a boat with a high stern. The body of the boat is painted yellow over a layer of plaster. Two steering oars are associated with this model, although it is very likely that one of them did not originally belong with this boat. The figure at the front of the boat might represent a sailor checking the depth of the water in which the boat is traveling.

Opposite:

EA 9525

Sycamore fig wood

Provenance unknown

12th Dynasty

Length 77.50 cm; Width 13.40 cm; Depth 6.00 cm

Purchased at the sale of the third Salt Collection in 1835

Literature: Glanville and Faulkner, *Wooden model boats*, 13-16, frontispiece, pl. IIIb (9).

This painted wooden model represents a funerary boat bearing a mummy on a bier beneath a canopy. To the port side of the mummy stands the small figure of a man, holding in his left hand a partially unrolled papyrus. He is presumably a lector-priest, who would read the ritual text written on the papyrus over the body. There are actually some traces of a text on the papyrus, but it has not been possible to read it. Fore and aft of the mummy stand two female mourners; these women are usually representations of Isis and Nephthys, the sisters of Osiris and archetypal mourners. At the rear, between a pair of steering oars, the helmsman is squatting. On the deck are also a small offering table and a couple of pots.

The body of the boat is painted green, as if to pretend that it was made of a material like papyrus, although in reality any such boat of this size could only have been made of wood. However, papyrus is symbolic of new life and rebirth and is appropriate for such a model to be placed in a tomb; the raised prow and stern are also elements from papyrus boats. Lotus (lily) flowers are painted on the paddles of the steering oars to give further emphasis to the associations with rebirth. The eye of Horus (*wedjat*), a symbol of healing and regeneration, is shown on the front of the body of the boat.

MODEL BOATS

Models became a common feature of Egyptian tomb contents in the later Old Kingdom through to the Middle Kingdom; in some cases the models augmented the depictions which were painted or carved onto tomb walls, but otherwise in effect replaced what was shown in such scenes.

Boats were particularly important models, judging from the number which has survived. They were of course the main means of transport in Egypt, and the Egyptians saw the sky as a celestial river, on which the sun god Re traveled every day in his own boat. In later times, owners of a *Book of the Dead* could join the sun god. In one spell in that text, the deceased must name all the elements of the boat before he can cross the celestial river to the Afterlife.

Boats in Egyptian tombs tend to occur in pairs, usually one with its sails set and the other propelled by oars. These different modes of navigation refer to the normal ways of traveling by river: as the prevailing wind was from the north, it helped boats traveling south against the current, while when traveling north, sails were not necessary because of the current. This was so fundamental to the Egyptian concept of travel that hieroglyphs reflecting these two different states were used in the words for "travel north" and "travel south."

Another important category of boat is the funerary boat, the central feature of which is a mummy on a bier. It is not clear whether this is a representation of the funeral of the deceased, when the body traveled from the land of the living (the east) to that of the dead (the west), or whether it could represent the wish for the pilgrimage journey to Abydos so the deceased could magically associate himself with Osiris. The latter scene becomes common in the painted decoration of tombs of the New Kingdom. The boats in this exhibit reflect the first and last of these types.

Literature:
Jones, *Boats*. See also Taylor, *Death and the afterlife*, 103-5.

MODEL OF A SERVANT FANNING FOOD

EA 29596

Wood, painted

Provenance unknown

6th-12th Dynasties, about 2200-1800 bc

Height 22.3 cm; Length 19.6 cm

Acquired in 1898

Unpublished. For comments on models see Taylor, *Death and the afterlife*, 99-103.

Figures of servants in tombs date back to the Old Kingdom, when they are found as individual stone statuettes. From the 6th Dynasty these begin to be replaced by figures in wood, and developed into groups of figures engaged in various tasks, often in models of the buildings in which they were to have worked. A wide variety of such models are found, ranging from butchers' and bakers' workshops through granaries to people carrying offerings, to model boats. Probably a majority of the figures are concerned with the production of food by magic for the deceased, and the butchers and bakers echo the importance of such scenes carved on the walls in Old Kingdom tombs. Many of these models come from burials with no associated decorated offering chapel, and it is quite likely that many were to some extent a less expensive substitute for painted or carved scenes. However, it must be noted that in the Middle Kingdom, officials who could afford painted tombs also had large quantities of models, as indeed was the case with the burial of king Mentuhotep II at Deir el-Bahari in Thebes. Thus it is also likely that these models, placed in close proximity to the body of the deceased, had important functions as servants for the dead, and it is perhaps possible that as they declined in popularity after the 12th Dynasty, their place was taken by the shabti.

This particular tomb-model represents a male servant squatting by a cooking fire, over which he is waving a fan. The figure is not part of a group, but is mounted on an individual base, perhaps an indication of a relatively early date, since these models became progressively more complex with the passage of time.

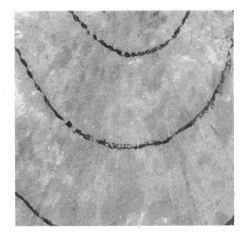

The wearing of gold jewelry, inlaid with precious stones and colored glass, was one of the principal ways of displaying one's high rank. To ensure that this status was perpetuated beyond death, jewelry was often placed in the grave with the mummy. The many elaborate collars and necklaces which were found in the tomb of Tutankhamun reveal the astonishing richness and variety of such costly pieces. They are also shown in paintings and on mummy cases as worn by non-royal persons, but because the actual items were major targets for tomb-robbers few well-preserved examples have been discovered in private burials. This fragment, said to have been found on a mummy in the Memphite necropolis in the early 19th century, is a rare survival. It is possible that the elements of which it is made originally formed parts of more than one object, but most of them would certainly have belonged to a collar.

The collar consisted of a series of rows of gold beads, attached to terminals in the shape of open lotus flowers. Each row was composed of beads of different shape, mainly imitating plant forms. There are folded leaves, papyrus flowers on stems, mandrake fruits alone and with leaves, flower buds, lotus seed-vessels and closed buds of the lotus. The terminal and beads are excellent examples of the cloisonné work, which was one of the favorite techniques of Egyptian goldsmiths. Most of the inlays have fallen out, but the tiny traces of cornelian and blue glass give a faint hint at the rich impression which the collar would have created in its pristine state.

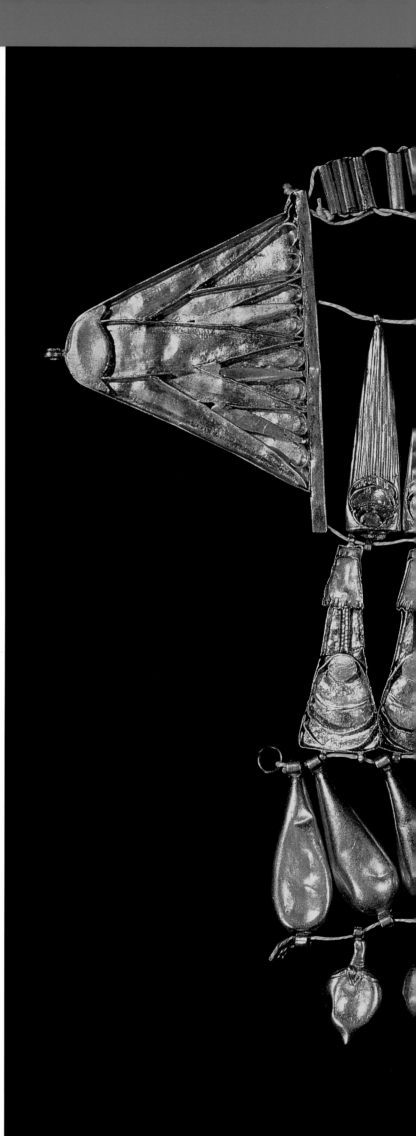

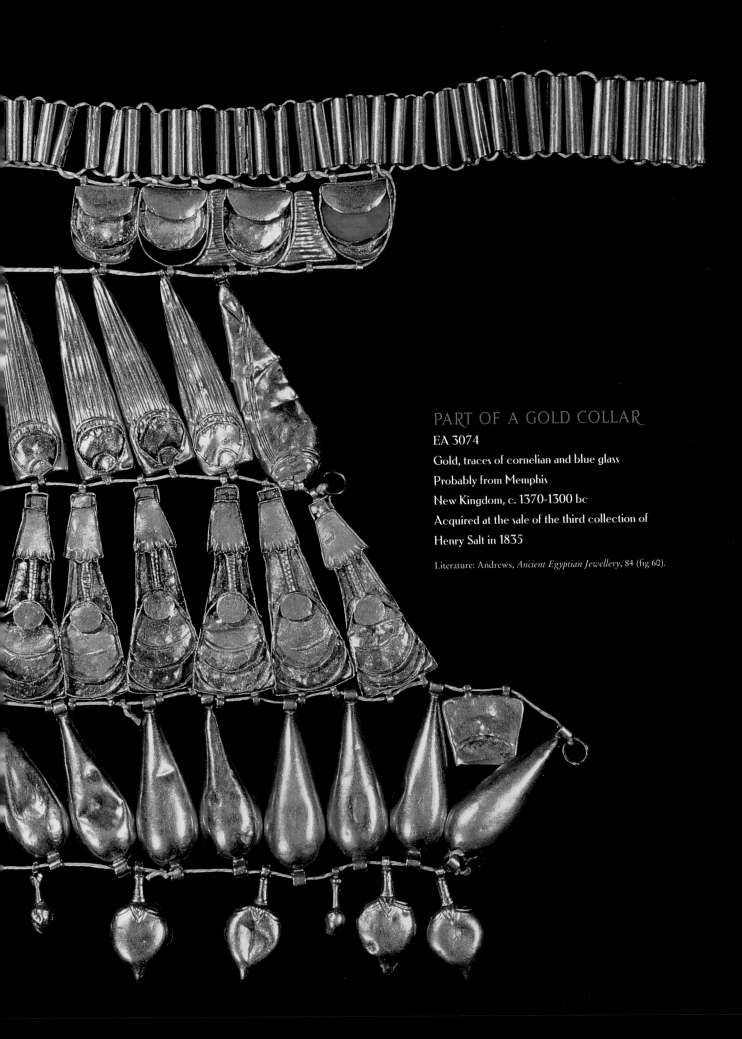

PART OF A GOLD COLLAR

EA 3074

Gold, traces of cornelian and blue glass

Probably from Memphis

New Kingdom, c. 1370-1300 bc

Acquired at the sale of the third collection of

Henry Salt in 1835

Literature: Andrews, *Ancient Egyptian Jewellery*, 84 (fig 60).

BRACELET

EA 3082

Electrum, semi-precious stones

Probably from Thebes

Middle Kingdom

Height 1.80 cm (spacers); Width 4.50 cm; Diameter 1.00 cm (beads spherical);

Length 23.80 cm (whole string)

Acquired at the sale of the third collection of Henry Salt in 1835

Published: Andrews, *Jewellery*, 74-5 (545), pl. 42; *Art and Afterlife in Ancient Egypt*, No 30.

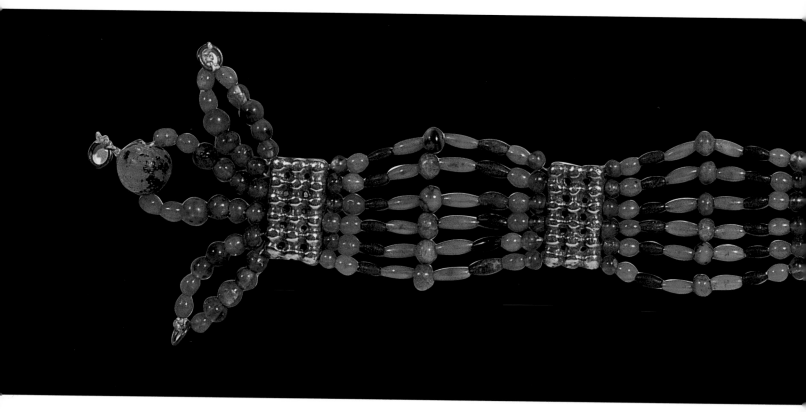

This bracelet is composed of six strings of stone beads threaded between five metal spacer-beads. The spacers, made in two halves, and decorated with horizontal and vertical knobs, represent multiple beads and are made of electrum (the one of gilded silver is perhaps modern); the object also comprises large spherical, oblate, spherical, standard and long truncated convex bicone beads of green glazed quartz, cornelian, amethyst, lapis lazuli, green feldspar and turquoise.

Although there are similarities to jewelry of the New Kingdom, the use of glazed quartz in this bracelet suggests that it is more likely to be of Middle Kingdom date.

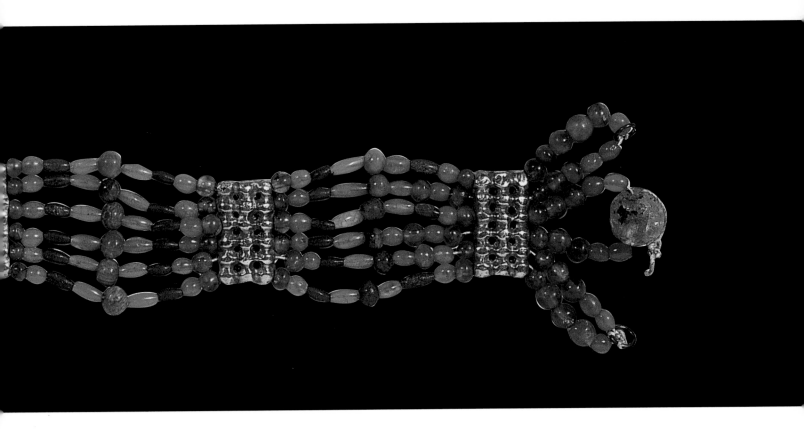

Rings with a bezel swivelling on a gold hoop are found in the New Kingdom and later. It is believed that the hoop of this ring is modern, but it quite accurately reflects the ancient mounting, along with the twist of fine gold wire beside the join with the bezel.

Both sides of the bezel bear incised decoration. One side shows a recumbent sphinx with a human head, wearing the so-called blue crown or cap, known as *khepresh,* and indicating that it represents the king. A cobra is shown behind the sphinx, giving its protection to the ruler; the smaller cobra on the royal brow, usually called a *uraeus,* is a royal symbol by which the dangerous power of the cobra is transferred to the king. In front of the sphinx is the hieroglyph *ankh* ("life"), expressing the wish, so commonly found in royal inscriptions, for life for the king.

The reverse side bears the figure of a goose adjoined by the name of the god Amun, and accompanied by the hieroglyph *nefer,* "perfection." The goose is a symbol of Amun, but as a hieroglyph it also means "son," and so the whole inscription may be interpreted as a wish for "perfection for the son of Amun."

FINGER RING

EA 4159

Faience and gold

Provenance unknown

18th Dynasty; hoop modern

Diameter 2.59 cm (hoop); Width 1.19 cm
(bezel); Length 1.75 cm (bezel);
Thickness 0.51 cm (bezel)

Acquired in 1840

Literature: Ziegler, *The Pharaohs,* 407, cat. 51 (picture incorrectly arranged with no 52); shown with a group of similar objects in Andrews, *Ancient Egyptian Jewellery,* fig. 146.

The first Egyptian earrings are seen in two-dimensional depictions and also in burials of women of the Middle Kingdom and Second Intermediate Period. Although the appearance of these ornaments might have coincided with the period of Hyksos control over parts of Egypt, it is now thought more likely that the Egyptians acquired the idea of ear ornamentation from the population of Nubia. Earrings seem to have been worn by both men and women, although women are shown more frequently with them.

It is unclear whether these two penannular earrings formed a pair. Although they reached the British Museum in the same year, they apparently came from two different sources. One of the earrings only has one attachment loop — and it does not appear that a second attachment loop is missing. These earrings are of a type known from the New Kingdom.

Both are made in two halves from a thick sheet of gold, shaped and then soldered together. At either end of the pennanular loop a further small piece of sheet gold was added to give the impression that the earrings were not hollow. The exterior seam on both is hidden by an applied band in the form of a rope plaited from three fine wires of gold; the interior seam was not further obscured. As observed, one has one circular loop at the end of the plait for fixing, while the other has two.

TWO
EARRINGS

EA 14350 and 14351

Gold

Provenance unknown

New Kingdom

Diameter 2.5-2.73 cm; Thickness 0.94 cm

Acquired in 1851

Unpublished. A similar object is illustrated in Andrews,
Ancient Egyptian Jewellery, fig. 91.

BEADS AND AMULETS STRUNG AS A NECKLACE

EA 24568

Gold, faience, cornelian

Probably from Thebes

Probably First Intermediate Period or Middle Kingdom

Length 54.60 cm

Acquired in 1889

Unpublished. For a string of beads with a *heh* amulet compare Andrews, *Jewellery I*, 48, pl. 22 (265). See Andrews, *Amulets* for further information about the amulets in the stringing.

This selection of beads and amulets has been strung in modern times into a necklace, although we cannot be sure of its original arrangement. In the present arrangement, sections of blue-green faience, cornelian and gold short cylinder, short truncated bicone and long bicone beads are strung between the amulets. The latter consist of seven *heh*-amulets of various dimensions, made of sheet gold and gold wire; two elaborate scorpion amulets made of gold; and two cornelian leg-amulets.

Each of these amulets had a magical function. The leg amulet was intended to ensure that the power of movement would remain with the wearer after death; it could even have been intended to replace by magic a limb which might become lost. The piece representing the scorpion would protect the wearer from the dangerous bite of that creature; as we see elsewhere with objects in this exhibition, the employment of the image of a feared animal could be turned around so as to enlist the danger inherent in that creature, or a god whom it represented, for the protection and empowerment of the deceased. The scorpion goddess was named Serqet, and is usually depicted as a woman with a scorpion on her head. The last amulet, the *heh*, takes as its form a composite hieroglyph of a squatting god with arms outstretched, holding in each hand the sign for "year"—together they represent the number "one million" and also the concept of "millions of years," and hence "eternity" or "infinity." Wearing these amulets on the body, perhaps strung round the neck (although we have no way of knowing if they all belong together), expressed a wish for protection, renewal and eternal life.

The leg amulet seems to be restricted to the Old Kingdom and the First Intermediate Period, while the *heh* is known from the end of the Old Kingdom to the Middle Kingdom. Strings of beads with these sorts of amulets have been excavated in sites in Middle Egypt such as Qau and Badari, where they are dated to the First Intermediate Period.

GOLD RING OF SHESHONQ

EA 68868

Provenance unknown, but perhaps from Thebes

26th Dynasty, 6th century bc

Diameter 3.00 cm; Length 3.40 cm (bezel)

Literature: *Egyptian Treasures* (Bowers Museum 2000): 226-227; shown with a group of similar objects in Andrews, *Ancient Egyptian Jewellery,* fig. 148. For further information on the Divine Adoratrice see Graefe, *Untersuchungen.*

This massive gold ring of Sheshonq is of a shape common for such rings in the Late Period, a shape which more or less totally replaced the earlier stirrup-shaped type. The lozenge shaped bezel is so thick that the back had to be cut away to accommodate the finger of the wearer; the shank and the bezel were made in separate molds and joined together. It is incised with the name of Sheshonq and his title "Chief Steward of the divine adoratrice." The bezel could be pressed into mud to seal documents and objects. Besides this functional aspect, the ring was no doubt as much (if not more) worn as a mark of Sheshonq's status and wealth.

The office of the "Divine Adoratrice of Amun" extends back into the late New Kingdom, but it became particularly important in Thebes during the Third Intermediate Period. At that time, the high priest of Amun was really more concerned with temporal power—he was the effective ruler of the area— and the Amun cult revolved around a woman appointed to the "Divine Adoratrice" post. These women were usually sisters or daughters of kings ruling in the north of Egypt, and by being placed in Thebes allowed those kings to keep a measure of influence there. They did not marry, and "adopted" their successors under the influence of the current king.

The name Sheshonq is of Libyan origin, belonging to several kings of the Libyan Period, but it became popular among Egyptians from that time onwards. Two men named Sheshonq are known as stewards of these women, and the limited information on this ring makes it difficult to know to which to ascribe it. The better-known Sheshonq, perhaps the more plausible candidate for the owner, who had an impressive tomb in the Assasif at Thebes, worked under the divine adoratrice Ankhnesneferibre, daughter of Psamtek II, in the first half of the 6th century *bc.* Statue EA 1162 in this exhibit is attributed to him. The other Sheshonq lived somewhat later, perhaps also in the lifetime of Ankhnesneferibre, but in the second half of the same century. The sarcophagus of Ankhnesneferibre and other material is in the British Museum. (see Section 1, The Gods, Object EA 1162).

A BEAD COLLAR

EA 41668

Faience

From Tomb 4 in the mortuary temple of Nebhepetre Mentuhotep
at Deir el-Bahari

11th Dynasty

Length 54.30 cm

Donated by the Egypt Exploration Fund in 1905

Literature: Andrews, *Jewellery I*, 60 (395). See Naville, *The XIth dynasty temple at Deir el-Bahari* I, 45-6 for information about the remainder of the burial. For notes on the "wives" of Mentuhotep, see Sabbahy, *Journal of the American Research Center in Egypt* 34 (1997), 163-6.

This broad collar is composed of one row of horizontally strung beads and five vertically strung rows, two semicircular terminals and fourteen mummiform pendants. The beads are a mixture of colors—bright blue, white and purple. The terminals, one of which is broken, have six holes in the straight side adjacent to the rest of the beads, and one hole in the rounded side, through which would have been threaded the material which permitted this to be hung round the neck. Many terminals from other periods are actually in the shape of falcon heads.

These collars are usually called "broad collars" by Egyptologists; the Egyptian term is *wesekh*. As with many items buried in the tomb, they could be understood on a number of different levels. Other than as simple adornment, the use of faience is highly symbolic of new life and rebirth; collars may also have had a particular ritual significance, as the *Book of the Dead* makes reference to a "spell for a golden collar to be placed on the throat of the deceased" (Spell 158).

This necklace, and one other very much like it in the British Museum (EA 40928), were found in subsidiary burials on the north side of the main platform of the mortuary temple/tomb of Nebhepetre Mentuhotep II, the 11th Dynasty king who reunified Egypt in about 2020 *bc*. The burials were located in simple chambers at the bottom of shafts, which showed evidence of reuse in the New Kingdom and Third Intermediate Periods. The name of the occupant of the tomb from which this collar comes, who was buried in a large rectangular limestone sarcophagus, is unknown, although all other burials in the area of this date were of women. Remains of more jewelry and some tomb models were also found. The named female burials were principally on the west side of the platform, and each had its own chapel, built during the earliest construction phase of the temple. These women were called "king's wives" in their chapel inscriptions but not in their burials, and this has led one scholar to suggest that they were "cultic" wives of the king when he was fulfilling a particular ritual role, that of the god Min. Hence they might have been a harem for him on earth, and were then buried in his mortuary temple. Although the owner of this necklace was not necessarily one of these women, she was presumably also of a very special status to have received a burial in this highly privileged temple location.

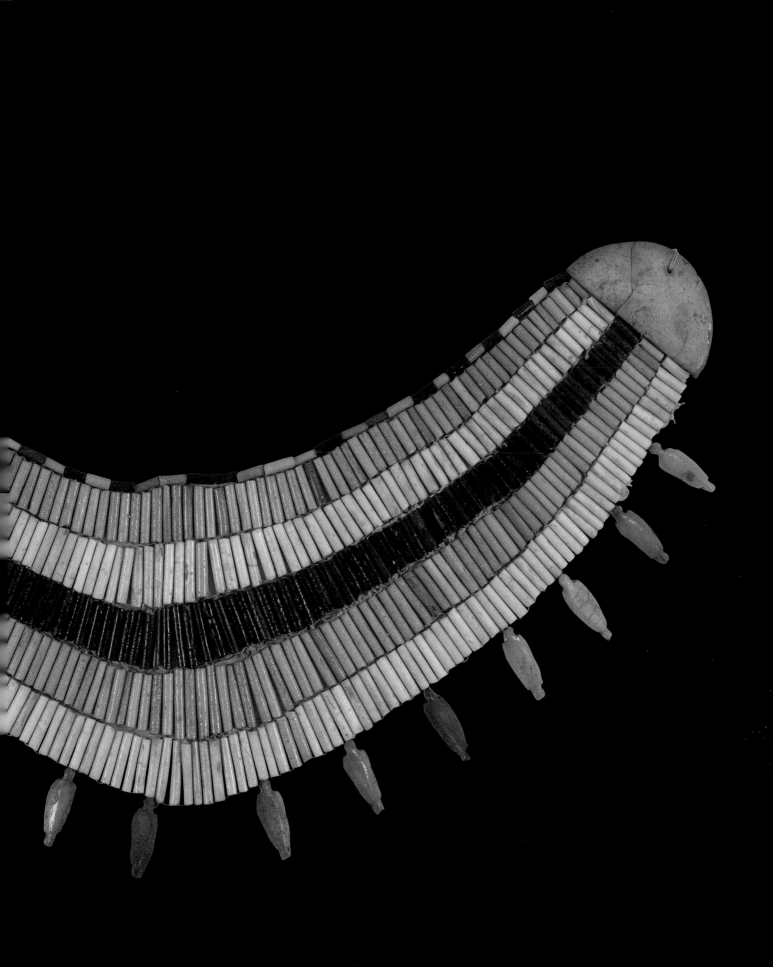

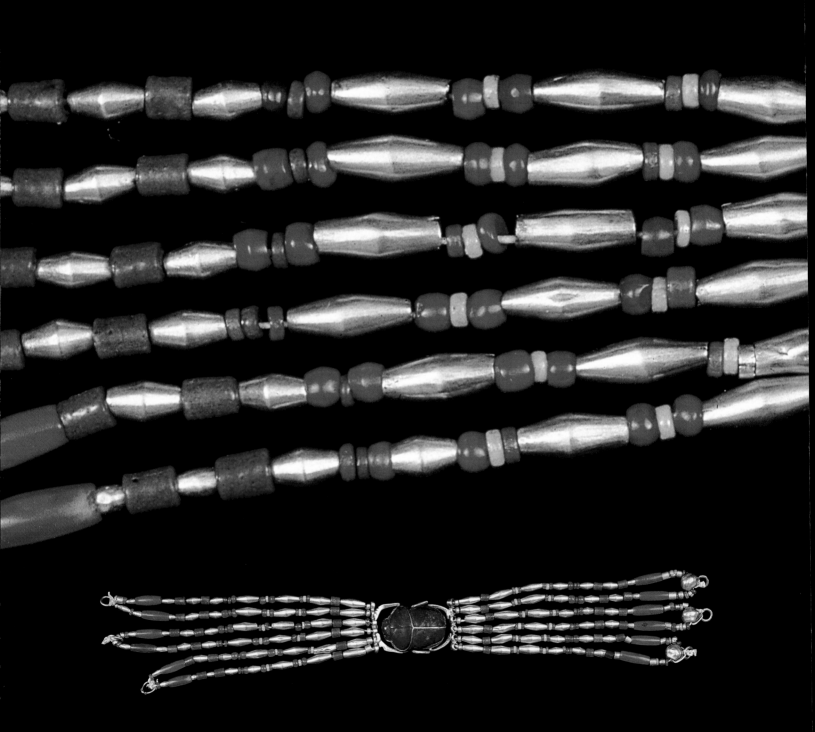

BRACELET WITH SCARAB

EA 65616

From Thebes

18th Dynasty

Width 1.60 cm (scarab); Length 2.90 cm; Length 19.50 cm

(bracelet as restrung)

Donated by Mrs. Essie Winifred Newberry in 1956

Literature: *Egyptian Treasures* (Bowers Museum 2000): 246-247. Illustrated:
Shaw & Nicholson, *British Museum Dictionary of Ancient Egypt*, 158.

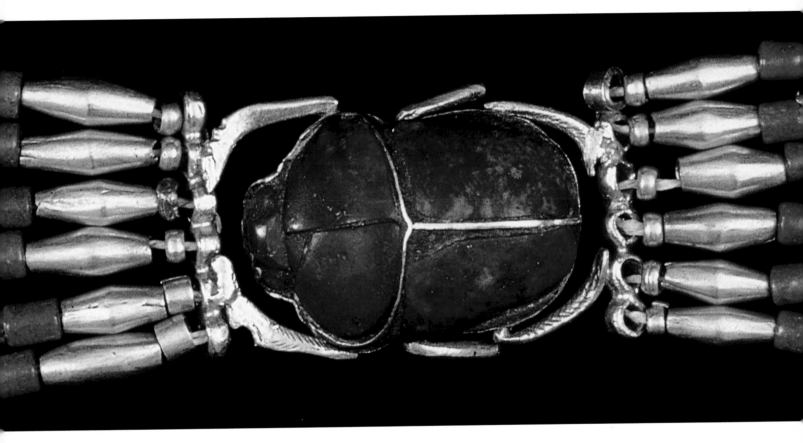

These beads and a scarab were originally found as loose elements but are now re-strung as a bracelet in the fashion of late 18th Dynasty royal jewelry. For this reason the Valley of the Kings has been suggested as a provenance. The variously shaped gold beads are formed from thin sheet metal folded over and joined along one edge. The large red beads near the end of the setting are of cornelian, while the smaller colored ones are of blue, red, yellow and green faience. The lapis lazuli scarab, with details of its back outlined in gold wire, is inset into a gold base, to which are soldered sheet gold legs carefully chased to indicate hairs. At the front and back it holds a bar of six gold rings to which are attached the stringing threads of the bead rows. Thus it acts as a spacer, a characteristic feature of Egyptian jewelry, intended to keep multiple strings taut and yet separate.

The manner in which the scarab rolls along a ball of dung in which it has laid its eggs gave rise to the idea that the sun traveled though the sky pushed by a giant scarab, and hence the insect was seen as a symbol of the sun. As the eggs inside the ball hatched, there arose the additional symbolic dimension that the insect represented new life, and indeed resurrection. This amuletic symbolism must explain why scarabs are not uncommonly found as elements of jewelry.

This gold finger ring consists of a thick circular hoop, supporting a square bezel with slightly rounded edges, inscribed with three lines of hieroglyphs. The content of the inscription is problematic, as the signs do not make any immediate sense, although this does not exclude the possibility that they conveyed some meaning in a very cryptic fashion. It has been suggested that the last line of signs may contain an unusual writing of the name Psamtek, perhaps commemorating a king of that name of the 26th Dynasty, but this is uncertain.

GOLD RING

EA 58937

Gold

Provenance unknown

Possibly 26th Dynasty

Diameter 2.62 cm (hoop); Length 2.34 cm (bezel);

Width 1.97 cm (bezel)

Donated by Sir Robert Ludwig Mond in 1927

Unpublished

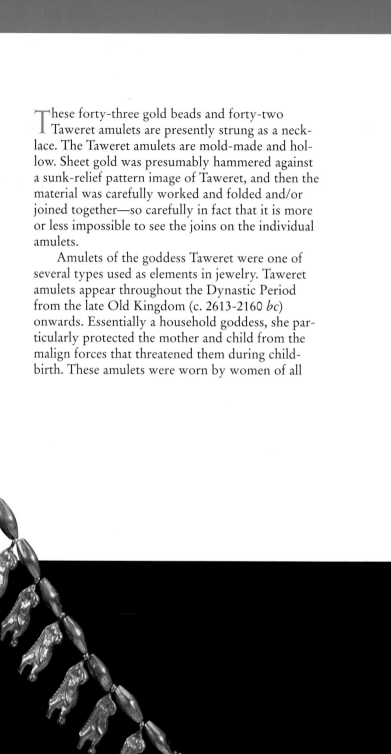

These forty-three gold beads and forty-two Taweret amulets are presently strung as a necklace. The Taweret amulets are mold-made and hollow. Sheet gold was presumably hammered against a sunk-relief pattern image of Taweret, and then the material was carefully worked and folded and/or joined together—so carefully in fact that it is more or less impossible to see the joins on the individual amulets.

Amulets of the goddess Taweret were one of several types used as elements in jewelry. Taweret amulets appear throughout the Dynastic Period from the late Old Kingdom (c. 2613-2160 *bc*) onwards. Essentially a household goddess, she particularly protected the mother and child from the malign forces that threatened them during childbirth. These amulets were worn by women of all

social groups. They were most often mass-pro-
duced and made of faience, but could also be carved
from various types of stone. A distinctive type in
red and black glass is characteristic of the 18th
Dynasty.

The present examples perhaps belonged to a
necklace, possibly to protect a woman during childbirth or to promote fertility. Some similar amulets,
there forming part of a collar, have been found in
burials of royal women of the New Kingdom,
including those of the foreign wives of king
Thutmose III. However, it cannot be assumed that
the original context of the present examples is
royal, since other amuletic necklaces of gold have
been found in private contexts, for example at
Sedment (in *Egypt's Golden Age* as above).

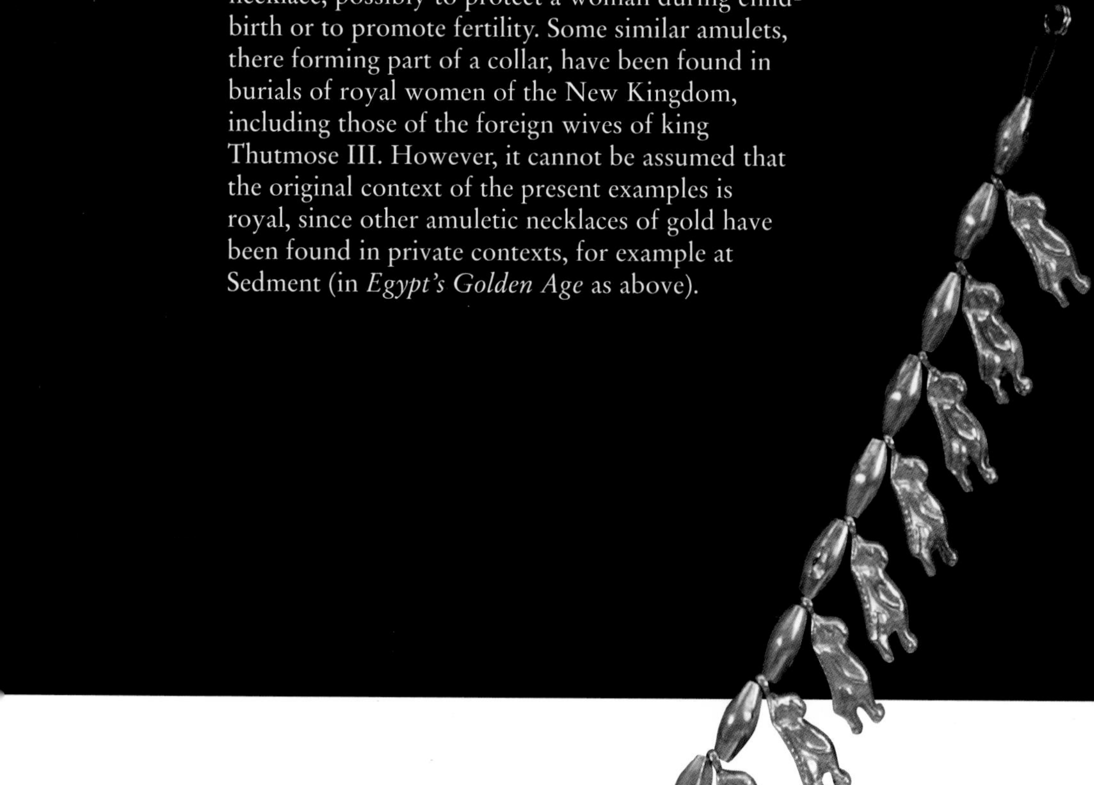

NECKLACE OF TAWERET AMULETS

EA 59418

Gold

Provenance unknown

18th Dynasty

Length 43.50 cm (as strung)

Gift of the members of the committee of the Egypt Exploration
Society from the collections of Sir John Maxwell in 1929

Literature: Quirke and Spencer, *The British Museum book of ancient Egypt*,
fig. 134; Andrews, *Amulets*, fig. 43e; *Gold and Civilisation*, Catalogue Australia
2001, 120. Similar amulets: Lilyquist, *The tomb of three foreign wives of
Tuthmosis III*, 174-5, 233; other amuletic necklaces, *Egypt's Golden Age*, 236-7.

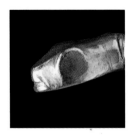

A PAIR OF BRACELETS

EA 34264

Gold and bronze or copper

Provenance unknown

Possibly New Kingdom or later

Diameter 7.50 cm

Acquired in 1901

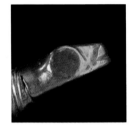

Pair of gold bracelets, made from twisted gold wire, apparently on a bronze or copper armature, with snake-headed terminals at the ends. The snake heads, in addition to being decorative, could also have an amuletic or protective function for the wearer. This would have extended into protection for the body after death, as it is likely that these came from a tomb.

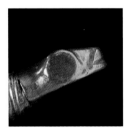

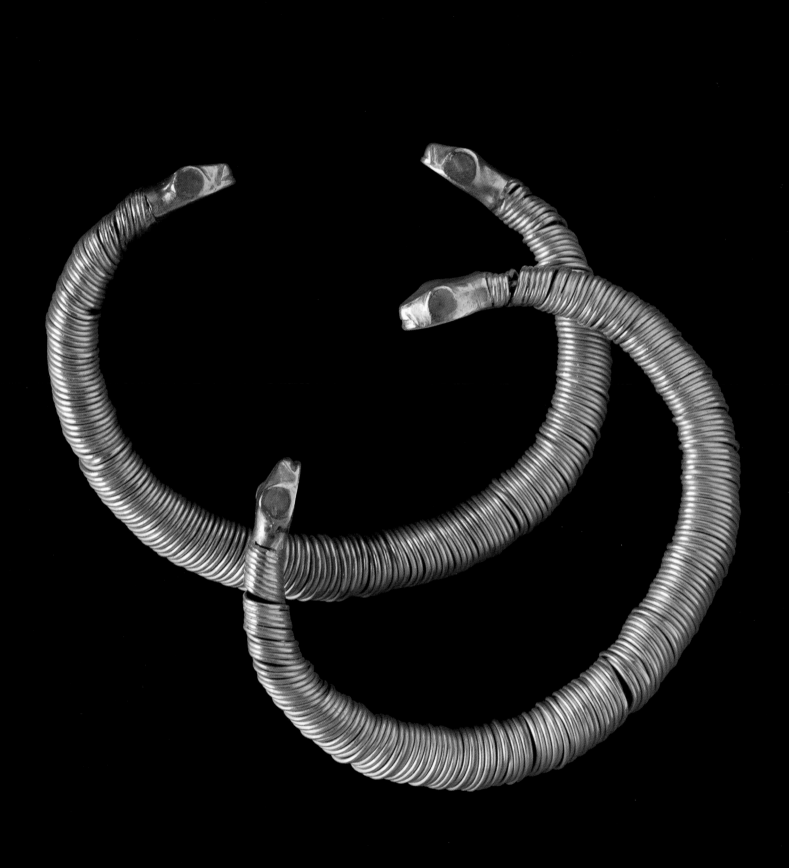

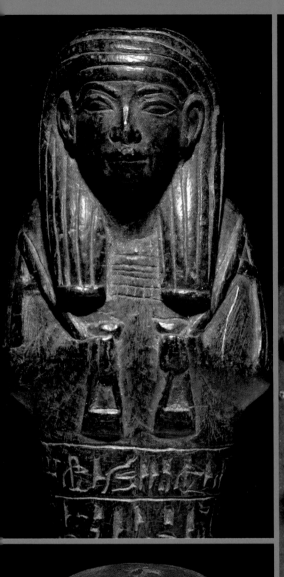

7

SERVANTS FOR THE AFTERLIFE

The Egyptian afterlife was conceived as a mirror of the real world, in which good and evil each had their place. The wicked were eternally punished, while the righteous enjoyed a comfortable existence journeying with the sun god or dwelling in the Field of Reeds. However, even the blessed dead would be subject to human needs and responsibilities, just as they had on earth. Thus the procurement of food and drink in the afterlife was a constant concern. For persons of high rank this challenge could be met through the offering cult and the provision of images of servants who would work for their masters eternally. On earth, these servants would also plant and harvest crops which the master owed to the king as taxes. But having deputies at one's command did not remove the *obligation* to work, a situation which was equally applicable to the realm of the dead. Here, as members of a hierarchical society ruled over by the gods, the dead could be called upon to labor in the fields, irrespective of their status.

The well-equipped Egyptian turned to magical assistance in order to avoid any unpleasant tasks that might be imposed on him after death. It was this concern which gave rise to one of the most distinctive features of Egyptian burial paraphernalia: the figurines known at different times by the names *shabti*, *shawabti* and *ushebti*. Made of stone, wood, pottery, faience and occasionally bronze, and ranging in height from a few centimetres to more than 0.5 meters, the figures represent the deceased as a mummy. The precise meaning of the first two names mentioned above is debatable; they have been compared with other Egyptian words meaning "stick," "persea tree" and "food," and it is possible that the names alluded either to the manufacture of the figures from wood or to their role as providers of sustenance for the deceased. The third word, *ushebti*, will be explained below.

They made their first appearance in the Middle Kingdom and functioned like other statues that were placed in the tomb, acting as substitute bodies in which the *ka* could dwell for eternity. Initially, then, the shabti fulfilled a role not unlike that of the *ka*-statue or even the mummy itself, as an eternal dwelling for the tomb-owner. But the *shabtis* also had a more specific duty, and this eventually became their chief function. The *shabti* was to take the owner's place when he was summoned by the gods to work in the fields of the netherworld. This concept is expressed in a spell which is first attested about 1900 *bc*, and which was eventually incorporated into the *Book of the Dead* as spell 6. In its simplest form, it states:

"O *shabti* allotted to me, if I be summoned or if I be detailed to do any work which has to be done in the realm of the dead; if indeed obstacles are implanted for you therewith, as a man at his duties, you shall detail yourself for me on every occasion of making arable the fields, of flooding the banks or of conveying sand from east to west; 'Here I am,' you shall say."

Although the wording of this text varied, the meaning is clear. When any onerous tasks were required of the deceased, the *shabti* would spring to life and answer the call. The spell was often inscribed on the body of the *shabtis* and, starting in the 18th Dynasty, they were even supplied with miniature agricultural tools (hoes and grain baskets) for their tasks. These items were sometimes individually made on a small scale, but more frequently they were carved or painted on the figurines. Another common text-formula written on shabtis gives the name of the owner preceded by the words *Sehedj Wsir*. This is a reference to the illumination of the dead person (equated with Osiris) by the life-giving rays of the sun, which symbolized his resurrection.

Once established as an essential item of tomb furniture, *shabtis* underwent stylistic evolution. Size, material, proportions, costume, implements and text all varied as fashions changed, and by plotting these fluctuations it is possible to date individual specimens accurately. There was also a gradual change in the magical function of the figures, reflected in the terminology applied to them, and in a steady increase in the quantity provided for each owner. In the Middle Kingdom there were only one or two figures per burial, but a high ranking official of the New Kingdom might own thirty or forty. At the end of the New Kingdom the workforce expanded to three hundred and sixty-five, one figure for each day of the year. They were supposed to operate in gangs of ten, and therefore a complete set also included thirty-six "overseers," equipped with whips to keep the workers at their tasks. By this date the figures were no longer regarded principally as manifestations of their own- ers. Now referred to as *hemu*, "slaves," they had become mere chattels, existing simply to do as they were ordered. At the same time, the standard terminology changed from *shabti/shawabti* to *ushebti*. This latter word denoted "one who answers," a further token of their subservient status. The need for larger numbers of figures led to a decline in quality. Many of those produced during the 1st millennium *bc* were mass produced in molds, and lack the aesthetic appeal of the individually crafted specimens of the New Kingdom. With the growing impact of Graeco-Roman customs on the elite of Egypt, burial practices changed, and in the Ptolemaic Period *ushebtis* ceased to be produced.

During the New Kingdom, the *shabtis'* role as substitutes for their owner led to their being sometimes deposited in places other than tombs. They have been found buried in groups at several religious centers, most importantly at Abydos, the burial place of Egypt's earliest kings and the cult center of the god Osiris. The deposition of *shabtis* in sacred spots such as these may have been intended to give their owners a symbolic presence at crucial religious festivals, such as that of Osiris. Perhaps, like the *ka*-statue in the tomb, the *shabti* enabled a person to receive a share of the offerings made to the gods.

Literature:
Taylor, *Death and the Afterlife*, 112-135.
Schneider, *Shabtis*

Opposite Page

MINIATURE COFFIN FOR A
SHABTI FIGURE OF TETI

EA 35016

Wood, painted

Provenance unknown

Second Intermediate Period, about 1600 bc

Height 14.3 cm; Width 10.2 cm; Length 29.5 cm

Acquired in 1868 from the collection of Robert Hay

This model is a close copy of the standard type of rectangular coffin used during the later Middle Kingdom and Second Intermediate Period. The use of such a container for a *shabti* emphasizes the close association which existed between the figurines and the deceased in the early phase of their use. At this stage, the *shabti* served essentially as a substitute for its dead owner and as such was buried with the same rites accorded to the corpse (the *shabti* was often wrapped in linen to imitate mummy-bandages). Good examples of *shabti* coffins of this period are those made for Bener and Wahneferhotep, found at Lisht.[1] This coffin, perhaps from Thebes, is simpler but it possesses several features that are particularly distinctive of its period, notably the large number of vertical inscriptions on the long sides and the figures of Isis and Nephthys at the ends – elements which appear on full-size coffins at the same date.

When the scribe wrote the inscriptions he evidently did not know for whom the coffin was to be used, and so in some places he put the words *men pen*, "this so-and-so," while leaving blank spaces elsewhere for the eventual insertion of the name. In two places the name Teti was added (though without erasing the *men pen*), and this name occurs again between two of the horizontal lines on the lid. Another remarkable feature characteristic of the Second Intermediate Period is that the scribe deliberately left certain hieroglyphic signs in the inscription incomplete. It is noticeable that all of the bird-signs are without legs. These "mutilated hieroglyphs" can be seen on other funerary objects, where (for example) the bodies of creatures such as snakes are intentionally cut through or truncated. This practice illustrates the Egyptians' belief in the power of an image to become reality; it was feared that pictures of dangerous creatures among the hieroglyphs might actually harm the deceased in the tomb, and so they were symbolically disabled to prevent this.

[1] Arnold, *The South Cemeteries of Lisht*, I: *The Pyramid of Senwosret I*, 34-6, 37-9, 147-9, pls. 11a, c, 13a, b, 14a, b.

SHABTI IN MINIATURE COFFIN

EA 65214

Provenance unknown

Mid-18th Dynasty, about 1450 bc

Coffin, painted wood: Height 8.9 cm; Width 8.4 cm; Length 25.7 cm

Shabti, painted and varnished wood: Length 18.6 cm; Width 4.2 cm

Acquired from the estate of Sir Robert Mond in 1939

During the early and middle years of the 18th Dynasty, private individuals usually possessed only a few *shabtis*. As befitted magical substitutes for their owners, these figures were treated like mummies and were often stored inside miniature coffins.

This group illustrates this practice. In its proportions the *shabti*-container faithfully reproduces those of an anthropoid (mummy-shaped) coffin of the middle 18th Dynasty, with a prominent foot and the sides of the case positioned at a steep angle to the horizontal. The exterior is painted yellow, perhaps to imitate the gold leaf with which the richest coffins would have been covered. This probably also explains why the painter has omitted the figures and inscriptions found on most full-sized coffins, although care has been taken to add the details of the face, wig and collar.

Four wooden pegs slotting into sockets along the edges enable the lid of the coffin to be held securely in place. When opened the *shabti* inside is revealed. It is a replica of the mummy, but its coloration, with yellow inscriptions on a black background, is taken from that of contemporary coffins and other funerary objects, a pattern of coloring which became fashionable in the reign of Tuthmosis III. The face is a reddish color and the entire surface of the figure has been liberally coated with a thick yellow varnish. Although the object can only be a shabti, it has neither the agricultural tools nor the appropriate spell from the *Book of the Dead*. The inscription is simply the age-old *hetep-di-nesu* formula: "An offering which the king gives to Osiris, lord of Djedu, the great god, ruler of eternity, that he might give an invocation offering of bread, beer, oxen and fowl for the ka of Djehuty."

This figurine, inscribed for a man named Nubyhat, is a good example of a well-crafted *shabti* dating from the mid-18th Dynasty. The "*shabti* spell" is incised in eight horizontal lines on the body; although the hands are depicted they hold no implements. These would only have come into fashion in succeeding generations.

SHABTI OF NUBYHAT

EA 64582

Wood

Provenance unknown

18th Dynasty

Height 23.0 cm; Width 7.10 cm

Gift of M.W. Acworth in 1946

SHABTI OF IPY

EA 27368

Steatite

Provenance unknown

Late 18th Dynasty, about 1370 bc

Height 11.1 cm; Width 3.9 cm

Acquired in 1896

This finely carved small *shabti* represents Ipy wearing a striated tripartite wig and a necklace. He holds a mattock and a hoe, carefully distinguished by the sculptor, and in each hand he also grasps a small bag or basket containing grain. These baskets began to appear as part of the equipment of the *shabti* in the late 18th Dynasty. At that time they were usually depicted on the front of the figure, held up by the *shabti* as if emphasizing its readiness to begin work, whereas on later examples they are shown on the back, slung over the shoulders on a cord. The seven horizontal lines of incised text on Ipy's figure contain part of the standard *shabti* spell.

SHABTI OF HUY

EA 34134

Painted wood

Provenance unknown

Late 18th Dynasty, about 1350 bc

Height 21.2 cm; Width 5.8 cm

Acquired in 1868 from the collection of Robert Hay

This *shabti* of the "Chief Doorkeeper of the Lord of the Two Lands" Huy is a small masterpiece of wood carving. The slender mummiform body has been exquisitely modeled and the details of the elaborately curled wig and the agricultural tools which Huy holds have been rendered in masterly fashion. The smoothed surface of the wood has been left unpainted for the most part, undoubtedly to emphasize the pattern of the grain. Against this ground the wig, facial features and details of the collar have been painted in contrasting black and white, and the incised hieroglyphs of the inscriptions were originally filled with a blue pigment. The long text in nine horizontal lines on the front of the body contains the *shabti*-spell, to ensure that the figure performed its tasks properly. The owner's name and title occur at the beginning, and these are repeated on the back of the *shabti* in a single vertical line. Huy's figure is well-equipped with a hoe and mattock and with a grain basket suspended from two cords on his back—all skillfully carved in shallow relief.

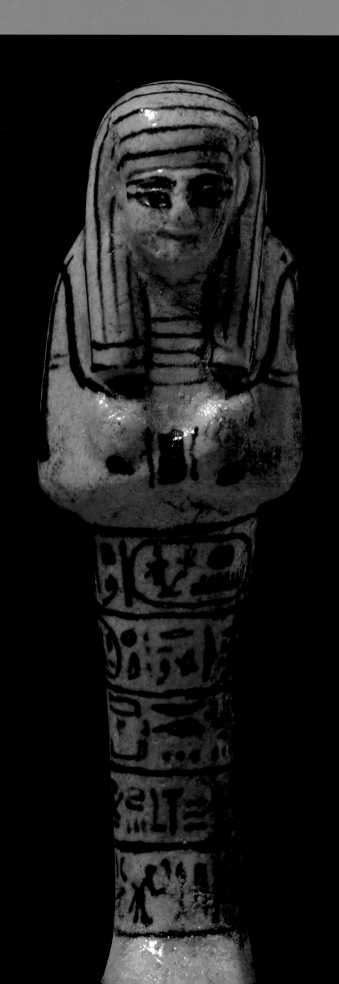

SHABTI OF KING SETY I

EA 8899

Blue-glazed faience

From the tomb of Sety I in the Valley of the Kings, Thebes

19th Dynasty, reign of Sety I, c. 1294-1279 bc

Height 15.2 cm; Width 4.8 cm

Acquired in 1837

The pharaohs expected that the exalted status they had enjoyed on earth would be maintained in the afterlife, but this did not necessarily mean that they would be exempt from laborious tasks. For this reason, kings as well as their subjects were provided with *shabti* figures. During the New Kingdom, when most burials contained only a few *shabtis*, the tombs of the pharaohs held hundreds of the figures. Sety I, whose tomb in the Valley of the Kings was one of the largest and most richly-decorated, possessed an exceptionally large number of *shabtis*.

This specimen is typical of the majority, which were made of wood or faience and were of modest size (c. 15-20 cm high) and routine workmanship. The decoration and inscription are in black on a turquoise-blue ground. The king is depicted in mummy shape and without any of the distinguishing trappings of royalty. Only his name, written within the cartouche, attests his high status. He wears a striated tripartite wig, a necklace and bracelets, and holds a hoe in each hand. A grain basket is slung over his shoulders, suspended on cords. A short version of the *shabti*-spell is inscribed around the lower part of the figure.

The hundreds of *shabtis* found in the tomb of
Tutankhamun illustrate an interesting diversity.
The majority are of modest size and their undistin-
guished workmanship shows that they were mass-
produced. But in addition to these humbler pieces,
the king possessed a limited number of large *shabtis*
of very high quality. Some of these bore dedicatory
inscriptions explaining that they were specially commissioned by high officials and donated to the king's
burial. This was a way of showing respect to the
dead ruler and perhaps also of sharing in some
manner his exalted afterlife through the medium of
the votive *shabti*.

Among the hundreds of *shabtis* that were placed
in the tomb of Sety I, there was also series of larger
figures of high quality. These were made of faience
and are distinguished by their skillful modeling and
the excellent quality of their blue glaze. None of the
surviving examples have votive texts mentioning
officials, yet the possibility exists that they were
gifts to the king, in the manner of the fine *shabtis*
of Tutankhamun.

It is to one of these larger *shabtis* that this head
belonged. It represents the king wearing the striped
nemes, or royal headcloth, here without the uraeus
serpent which usually rears up at the brow. From
more complete examples it can be deduced that the
king also wore an elaborate collar and bracelets, and
grasped two hoes in his crossed hands. The standard
shabti-spell would have been inscribed in horizontal
lines around the body and legs.

HEAD OF A SHABTI OF KING SETY I

EA 9216

Blue-glazed faience

From the tomb of Sety I in the Valley of the Kings, Thebes

19th Dynasty, reign of Sety I, c. 1294-1279 bc

Height 5.5 cm; Width 7.75 cm

Acquired in 1842

This small stone *shabti* depicts its owner Khatemwia wearing a simple tripartite wig and holding a hoe in each hand. It is of simple but competent workmanship, with flesh and hoes painted red, and wig, facial details and inscription colored black. The text, inscribed in four lines, is a short version of the *shabti* spell; it lacks the phrases in which the *shabti* is instructed to work on behalf of its owner—yet according to ancient Egyptian notions this would not impair its functioning. Long religious inscriptions, written on coffins, statuettes and amulets, were often represented by only a part of the text—this part, it was believed, would work just as effectively as the whole.

SHABTI OF KHATEMWIA

EA 35367

Limestone, painted

Provenance unknown

19th Dynasty, about 1295-1186 bc

Height 13.2 cm; Width 5.0 cm

Acquired in 1901

In the later 18th Dynasty there was a move away from the fashion of depicting the dead as mummies and towards representing them as living beings dressed in formal clothes. This led to the creation of coffins, sarcophagi and *shabtis* in this form, although the more traditional shrouded image continued to be used at the same time.

This *shabti* of the Overseer of the Granary Amenwahsu exemplifies this trend. He wears the curled double wig and the pleated kilt with prominent apron that were fashionable dress for high officials at the time. His arms and legs are free from the confining mummy-wrappings. He holds a hoe in each hand and has a grain-basket slung over his left shoulder. The *shabti*-spell is inscribed in horizontal lines, but its positioning around the back and sides seems deliberately to reduce its prominence, giving greater emphasis to the sculptural qualities of the figure.

SHABTI OF
AMENWAHSU

EA 53972

Steatite

Provenance unknown

19th Dynasty, about 1295-1186 bc

Height 18.9 cm; Width 7.22 cm

Acquired in 1915

Merienset, "The Beloved of the god Seth," probably owned several wooden *shabtis* of similar design. The body is white, suggesting the brilliant linen shroud that was appropriate to the dead. Over this is a large collar, colored blue, green, red and yellow. The arms are crossed and the hands are shown protruding through the lower rows of the collar—a graphic peculiarity which also appears on mummiform coffins in the 19th and 20th Dynasties. The painter seems to have decided not to try to superimpose agricultural tools on the polychrome collar, where perhaps they would have lacked clarity. Instead, he left the hands empty and painted the two hoes on the back of the figure, where they appear "floating" rather incongruously on each side of a large grain basket hanging on cords. The design of the figure was completed by a single line of inscription on the front, introducing the name of the owner as *sehedj* and adding the opening words of the *shabti* spell without detailing any of the specific tasks that the figure was required to perform.

WOODEN SHABTI
OF MERIENSET

EA 30804

Painted wood

Provenance unknown

19th Dynasty

Height 19.5 cm; Width 6.0 cm

Acquired in 1899

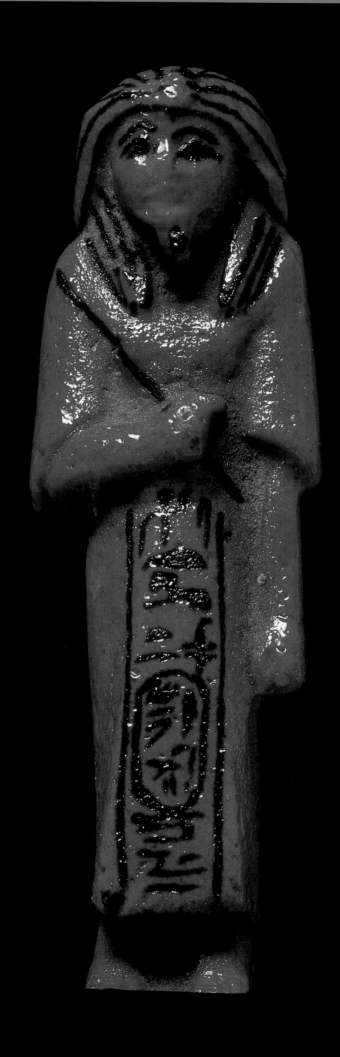

OVERSEER SHABTI OF KING PINEDJEM I

EA 18588

Faience

From the "Royal Cache," Deir el-Bahari

21st Dynasty, about 1070-1032 bc

Height 12.6 cm; Width 4.0 cm

Acquired in 1887

Literature: *Egyptian Treasures* (Bowers Museum 2000), 162-3
(erroneously called "Pinedjem II").

This shabti comes from the burial of Pinedjem I. He was high priest of Amun and army commander at Thebes in the early 21st Dynasty—posts which gave him virtual control of the whole of southern Upper Egypt. During his rule he organized the transfer of many of the mummies of the New Kingdom pharaohs from their tombs to inconspicuous and easily-guarded caches, and it was in the largest of these, the "Royal Cache" at Deir el-Bahri, that he himself was ultimately buried. On the basis of his powerful position he adopted the titles and trappings of kingship on some of his monuments. This is particularly apparent on his burial equipment, where his name is written in a cartouche and he wears the royal uraeus serpent on his headdress. Pinedjem's shabtis are made of deep blue-glazed faience with details in black paint. They are divided into "overseer" and "worker" types. This is a typical overseer; the individual is dressed in a wig and a robe of the type worn by the living. His right arm is flexed across his chest and holds a stylized whip, ready to bring down on the backs of any reluctant workers. The short text on his apron identifies him as the *sehedj*, the Osiris-king Pinedjem, beloved of Amun.

SHABTI BOX

EA 22820

Provenance unknown, probably from Thebes

25th Dynasty

Height 21.00 cm; Width 13.5 cm; Length 27.5 cm

Acquired in 1891

By the 25th Dynasty the quality of *shabtis* had declined dramatically—even those made for high-ranking individuals at Thebes were very small and crudely modeled, without any of the detail or refinement of their counterparts in earlier periods. The majority of these figures were uninscribed, lacking even the owner's name. They were usually heaped unceremoniously into wooden boxes which were placed at the side of the coffin.

This box is a typical *shabti*-container of the 25th Dynasty. It is painted white with a flat lid on which a boat is painted. The projecting end boards are rounded off, and the simple inscription gives only the owner's name and filiation. He was a Chief Singer of the Domain of Amun named Iryiry, and his father had held the same title. This information, together with the style of the box, strongly suggests that Iryiry worked in the temple of Karnak and that his tomb (now unidentifiable) was located on the Theban west bank. In the later New Kingdom, *shabti* boxes usually imitated the appearance of shrines, with vaulted lids and tapering sides. But in the Third Intermediate Period the status of *shabtis* changed; they ceased to be in some way the embodiment of the deceased owner and came to be regarded simply as his or her slaves. They were no longer images of the deceased in a divine state and perhaps for this reason it was not considered appropriate for their containers to represent shrines, the receptacles for divine beings—the boxes therefore assumed more mundane forms.

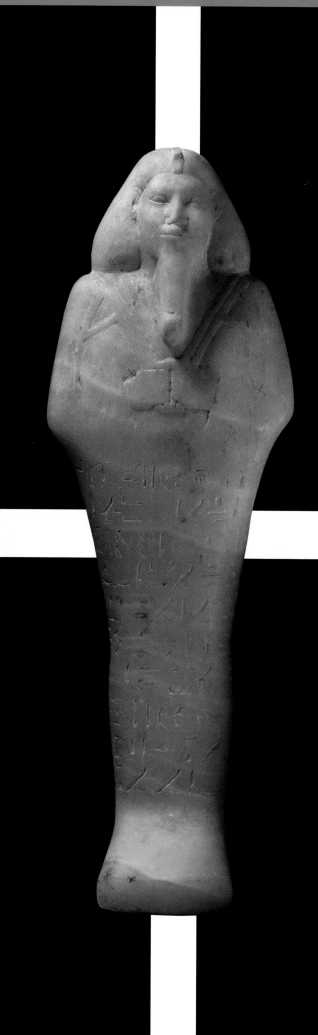

SHABTI FIGURE OF KING TAHARQA

EA 55483

Egyptian alabaster

From the pyramid of Taharka at Nuri, Sudan, excavated by G.A. Reisner

25th Dynasty, reign of Taharqa, 690-664 bc

Height 33.5 cm

Donated by the government of Sudan in 1922.

Literature: Dunham, *The Royal Cemeteries of Kush*, II: *Nuri*, 10, fig 197, pl. CXL.

After a decline in quality, *shabtis* underwent a revival in the 25th-26th Dynasties. This development was part of a general trend in Egypt towards archaism, which was manifested in art, architecture and literature as well as burial customs. The tendency was given great impetus under the Kushite rulers who controlled both Egypt and the Sudan in the late 8th and early 7th century *bc*. They adopted pharaonic burial practices including mummification of the king's body and interment beneath a pyramid. Large numbers of *shabtis* were also placed in these royal graves. The greatest of the Kushite pharaohs, Taharqa, possessed at least one thousand and seventy, which were placed standing in rows in the chambers and passages of his tomb.

The *shabtis* of Taharqa exemplify the desire of these Kushite kings to draw inspiration from the great ages of Egypt's past. They are of exceptionally large size, and are carved from a variety of stones—granite, calcite and ankerite. In this, and in their rugged, strongly-marked sculptural qualities, the figures recall the large stone *shabtis* of the Middle and New Kingdoms. The reliance on older models is also apparent in the text of the *shabti* spell, inscribed around the king's body. It is based on much earlier versions, with unusually full wording in place of the abbreviated texts that had been in fashion in the Third Intermediate Period.

USHEBTI OF PSAMTEK, SON OF SEBAREKHYT

EA 49420

Faience

From Saqqara

26th Dynasty

Height 18.6 cm; Width 5.1 cm

Acquired in 1910

The official Psamtek, son of a woman named Sebarekhyt, possessed an unusually fine set of ushebtis in bright blue-glazed faience. His tomb was situated at Saqqara, but its precise location is now lost; many objects from it entered European museums and collections in the 19th century.

Psamtek holds a hoe in his right hand and a pick in his left. A basket on a cord hangs over his left shoulder. An inscription in eight horizontal lines contains the ushebti spell.

USHEBTIS OF THE LATE PERIOD

A new standard type of ushebti was introduced at the beginning of the 26th
Dynasty, continuing in use until the Ptolemaic
Period. Usually made from green or blue-
glazed faience, these figurines are recognizable
by their slender proportions, long wig and
beard and by the addition of features which
are commonly found on stone sculpture – a
plinth under the feet and a pillar supporting
the back. Most of these ushebtis hold a pair of
hoes or a hoe and pick, with a basket suspended over the shoulder on a cord. As in earlier
periods, the body is generally occupied by
inscriptions, here either the ushebti spell in
horizontal lines or the name and parentage of
the owner in a vertical line.

USHEBTI OF HOR

EA 34102

Faience

Provenance unknown

26th Dynasty

Height 18.8 cm; Width 5.6 cm

Acquired in 1853

This ushebti is a fine example of the
style of the 26th Dynasty. Its surface
glaze, originally green, has partly disappeared leaving a brown patination.
Hor is described as a King's Scribe,
and his mother's name, Merneit, is
also recorded. The inscription contains the ushebti spell.

USHEBTIS OF THE LADY TARUDET

EA 9175-9181
EA 9183
EA 9184
EA 9186
Faience
Probably from Saqqara
27th-30th Dynasties
Heights 13.0-15.9 cm

A standard set of *ushebtis* in the Late Period numbered four hundred and one figures. This total comprised three hundred and sixty-five "worker" *ushebtis*, with thirty-six "overseers" (one to control every ten workers). In earlier centuries the two types of figures differed in appearance. Now the distinction was no longer reflected in the iconography of the statuettes, yet stylistic variation can be observed among the *ushebtis* made for a single owner. These green-glazed faience *ushebtis* of Tarudet, daughter of Ta-amen, are a case in point. All of them have essentially the same form, with pedestal and back-pillar, hoe, mattock and grain-basket. They are also bearded, showing that the divine image on which they are modeled was more influential than any aim of representing the individual owner, in this case a woman. The figures would have been made in molds, offering the possibility of producing many identical castings. Yet each figure has slightly different dimensions from its fellows and in the inscriptions there are small variations in the shaping of the hieroglyphic signs and in the spelling of the names, showing that each was molded individually. The text is the simple *sehedj* formula. On some of the *ushebtis* it is written in a horizontal and vertical line, on others in a vertical line only. On two of the latter, however, the word *sehedj* was omitted from the central column of text and was added rather clumsily at the side.

These *ushebtis* must have been among the earliest to find their way to Europe. During the 17th and 18th centuries *ad* travel to Egypt was hazardous due to the risk of plague and the hostility of the inhabitants to foreigners. Few European travelers penetrated Upper Egypt at this time, and most were content to visit the pyramids and the adjacent tombs at Giza and Saqqara. The majority of the antiquities brought back to Europe at that time came from the more easily accessible Late Period tombs and sacred animal catacombs at the latter site. One of the burials that evidently was accessible to collectors was that of Tarudet. An *ushebti* bearing her name was presented to the Bodleian Library, Oxford, by Archbishop William Laud as early as 1635. Those displayed here formed part of the collection of the merchant Pitt Lethieullier, assembled in the early 18th century and given to the British Museum in 1756.

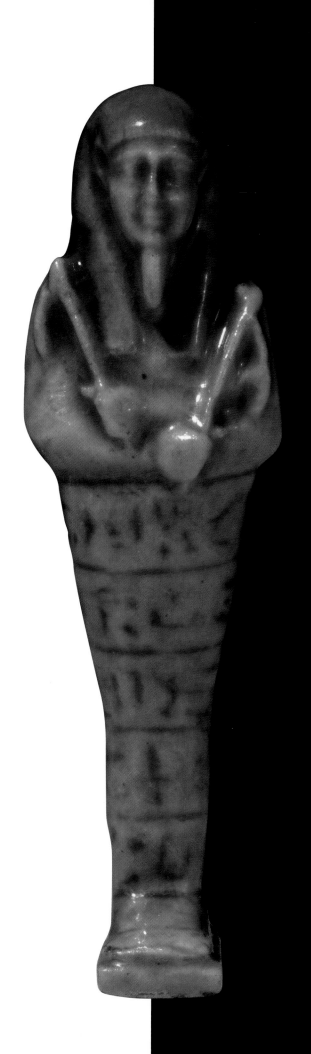

TWO-TONE SHABTI OF PETOSIRIS

EA 37332

Blue-glazed faience

From Abydos, Petrie's Cemetery G, tomb 50

Early Ptolemaic Period, about 250 bc

Height 12.4 cm; Width 3.8 cm

Gift of Egypt Exploration Fund in 1902

Literature: Petrie, *Abydos* I, 39, pl. LXXIX, 2, middle right; Aubert and Aubert, *Statuettes Égyptiennes, Chaouabtis, Ouchebtis*, 265-6, 282.

By the beginning of the Ptolemaic Period, the production of shabtis had begun to go into decline. The basic form and iconography of the figures which had been established in the 26th Dynasty, with back-pillar and pedestal, continued, but there were few significant developments in design. Among the last innovations of any note was the use of a two-tone coloration. The wig and inscriptions were colored deep blue, which stood out against a pale blue background. The surface was thickly vitrified; this gave the shabti a luminescent quality, although it also had the unfortunate effect of making the inscriptions appear rather blurred and indistinct.

This new coloring is exemplified by the shabti of Petosiris. This individual was a priest of the goddesses Hathor and Wadjit (the titles are attested on other, more clearly legible shabtis). He was buried together with his parents and two of his brothers in a two-chambered family tomb at Abydos.[1] Inside the vaulted sepulcher, sand had been heaped over the sarcophagi of the three occupants. Canopic chests had been placed on the top of this fill, and most of the shabtis of Petosiris were discovered lying loose within the sand. In total, three hundred and eighty-five shabtis of different sizes belonging to Petosiris were found; thirty-six of these were inscribed with spell 6 of the *Book of the Dead*. It is conceivable that these represent the thirty-six "overseers" traditionally required for a full set, and that the plain shabtis were the "workers." The adjacent chamber contained the burial of Petosiris' father Djedher. Interestingly, the shabtis of the father, though crudely modeled, were of the more traditional type with a uniform blue-green glaze; this may indicate that Petosiris' two-tone shabtis were among the first of their type.

[1] For the tomb and burials of Djedhor and his family: Petrie, *Abydos* I, 37-39, pl. LXXV-LXXX; Porter and Moss, V, 75).

BIBLIOGRAPHY

Ägyptens Aufstieg zur Weltmacht. Exhibition Catalogue, Hildesheim 1987 (Hildesheim and Mainz 1987).

Andrews, C, *Amulets of Ancient Egypt* (London 1994).

Andrews, C, *Ancient Egyptian Jewellery* (London 1996).

Andrews, C, *Egyptian Mummies.* Second edition (London 1998).

Andrews, C, *Jewellery I. From the Earliest Times to the Seventeenth Dynasty.* Catalogue of Egyptian Antiquities in the British Museum, 6. (London 1981).

Arnold, D, *The Encyclopaedia of Ancient Egyptian Architecture* (London 2003).

Arnold, D, *The Pyramid of Senwosret I.* The south cemeteries of Lisht I (New York 1988).

Art and Afterlife in Ancient Egypt: From the British Museum. Exhibition Catalogue, Japan 1999-2000 (1999).

Aston, B G, *Ancient Egyptian Stone Vessels. Materials and Forms.* Studien zur Archäologie und Geschichte Altägyptens, 5 (Heidelberg 1994).

Aston, B G, Harrell, J A, and Shaw, I, "Resins, amber and bitumen," in Nicholson and Shaw (eds), *Ancient Egyptian Materials and Technologies,* 430-74.

Aubert, J-F, and L, *Statuettes égyptiennes, Chaouabtis, ouchebtis* (Paris 1974).

Bianchi, R S, "Those Ubiquitous Glass Inlays from Pharaonic Egypt. Suggestions about Their Functions and Dates," *Journal of Glass Studies* 25 (1983), 29-35.

Bianchi, R S, "Those Ubiquitous Glass Inlays, Part II," *Bulletin of the Egyptological Seminar of New York* 5 (1983), 9-29.

British Museum, *A Guide to the First and Second Egyptian Rooms,* 2nd ed. (1904).

Bryan, B M, "The statue program for the mortuary temple of Amenhotep III," in Quirke, S, (ed.), *The temple in Ancient Egypt. New discoveries and recent research* (London 1997), 57-81.

Budge, E A W, *The Greenfield Papyrus in the British Museum* (London 1912).

Buhl, M-L, *The Late Egyptian Anthropoid Stone Sarcophagi* (Copenhagen 1959).

Cooney, J D, *Glass*. Catalogue of Egyptian Antiquities in the British Museum, 4 (London 1976).

Corcoran, L H, *Portrait Mummies from Roman Egypt (I-IV Centuries A.D.)*. Studies in Ancient Oriental Civilization, 56. (Chicago 1995).

d'Athanasi, G, *A brief account of the researches and discoveries in Upper Egypt made under the direction of Henry Salt* (London Hearne 1836).

D'Auria, S, Lacovara, P, Roehrig, C H, *Mummies & Magic. The Funerary Arts of Ancient Egypt*. Exhibition Catalogue, Boston, Museum of Fine Arts (Boston 1988).

Davies, W V, "Ancient Egyptian timber imports. An analysis of wooden coffins in the British Museum," in Davies, W V, and Schofield, L, (eds), *Egypt, the Aegean and the Levant. Interconnections in the Second Millennium BC.* (London 1995).

Davies, W V, *A Royal Statue Reattributed*. British Museum Occasional Paper 28. (London 1981).

Dawson, W R, and Gray, P H K, *Mummies and Human Remains*. Catalogue of Egyptian Antiquities in the British Museum, 1. (London 1968).

Des Dieux, des tombeaux, un savant. En Egypte sur les pas de Mariette Pacha. Exhibition Catalogue, Boulogne 2004 (Paris 2004).

Doxiadis, E, *The Mysterious Fayum Portraits. Faces from Ancient Egypt* (London and New York 1995).

Dunham, D, *The Royal Cemeteries of Kush*. II, *Nuri* (Boston 1955).

Egypt's Golden Age. The Art of Living in the New Kingdom. 1558-1085 B.C. Exhibition Catalogue, Boston, Museum of Fine Arts, 1982 (Boston 1982).

Egyptian art in the age of the Pyramids. Exhibition Catalogue, New York 1999-2000 (New York 1999).

Egyptian Treasures from the British Museum. Exhibition Catalogue, Bowers Museum 2000 (Santa Ana 2000).

el-Sadeek, W, *Twenty-Sixth Dynasty Necropolis at Gizeh. An Analysis of the Tomb of Thery and its Place in the Development of Saite Funerary Art and Architecture*. Veröffentlichungen der Institute für Afrikanistik und Ägyptologie der Universität Wien 29 (Vienna 1984).

Faulkner, R O, *The Ancient Egyptian Book of the Dead*. Edited by C, Andrews. (London 1985).

Filer, J M, "If the Face Fits ... A Comparison of Mummies and their Accompanying Portraits Using Computerised Axial Tomography," in Bierbrier, M L, (ed.), *Portraits and Masks. Burial Customs in Roman Egypt* (London 1997), 121-6.

Franke, D, *Personendaten aus dem Mittleren Reich (20.-16. Jahrhundert v. Chr.). Dossiers 1-976*. Ägyptologische Abhandlungen 41 (Wiesbaden 1984).

Friedman, F D, *Gifts of the Nile. Ancient Egyptian Faience*. Exhibition Catalogue, Providence and Fort Worth 1998-9 (Providence and London 1998).

Glanville, S R, and Faulkner, R O, *Wooden model boats*. Catalogue of Egyptian Antiquities in the British Museum, 2 (London 1972).

Gold and Civilisation, Exhibition Catalogue, Australia 2001 (Sydney and Canberra 2001).

Graefe, E, *Untersuchungen zur Verwaltung und Geschichte der Institution der Gottesgemahlin des Amun vom Beginn des Neuen Reiches bis zur Spätzeit.* Ägyptologische Abhandlungen 37. Wiesbaden.

Grajetzki, W, *Burial Customs in Ancient Egypt.* (London 2003).

Grallert, S, "Die Fugeninschriften auf Sargen des Mittleren Reiches," *Studien zur Altägyptischen Kultur* 23 (1996), 147-165.

Grimm, G, *Die römischen Mumienmasken aus Ägypten.* Wiesbaden.

Hart, G, *A Dictionary of Egyptian Gods and Goddesses* (London, Boston and Henley 1986).

Haynes, J L, "The Development of Women's Hairstyles in Dynasty Eighteen," *Journal of the Society for the Study of Egyptian Antiquities* 8 (1977-78), 18-24.

Helck, W, *Zur Verwaltung des Mittleren und Neuen Reichs.* Probleme der Agyptologie 3 (Leiden-Cologne 1958).

Hieroglyphic Texts from Egyptian Stelae etc. [British Museum]. 12 parts (London 1911-93).

Hölscher, U, *The Mortuary Temple of Ramses III. Part II.* The Excavation of Medinet Habu, Volume IV (Chicago 1951).

Hölzl, C, (ed.), *Die Pyramide Ägyptens.* Exhibition Catalogue, Schallaburg 2004 (Vienna 2004).

Hornung, E, *Conceptions of God in Ancient Egypt. The One and the Many* (London, Melbourne and Henley 1982).

Ikram, S, and Dodson, A, *The mummy in Ancient Egypt. Equipping the Dead for Eternity* (London 1998).

James, T G H, *Egyptian Painting* (London 1985).

Jones, D, *Boats.* (London 1995).

Journal of Egyptian Archaeology, 57 (1971).

Killen, G, *Ancient Egyptian Furniture. Vol. I. 4000-1300 B.C.* (Warminster 1980).

Kitchen, K A, *Ramesside Inscriptions. Historical and Biographical. III* (Oxford 1980).

Kozloff, A, and Bryan, B M, *Egypt's Dazzling Sun. Amenhotep III and his World.* Exhibition Catalogue Cleveland and Fort Worth 1992 (Cleveland 1992).

Lapp, G, *Typologie der Särge und Sargkammern von der 6. bis 13. Dynastie.* Studien zur Archäologie und Geschichte Altägyptens 7 (Heidelberg 1993).

Lilyquist, C, *Egyptian Stone Vessels. Khian through Tuthmosis IV* (New York 1995).

Lilyquist, C, *The tomb of three foreign wives of Tuthmosis III* (New York 2003).

Lucas, A, *Ancient Egyptian Materials and Industries.* Fourth Edition, revised and enlarged by J R Harris (London 1962).

Müller-Winkler, C, *Die ägyptischen Objekt-Amulette*. Orbis Biblicus et Orientalis, Series Archaeologica 5 (Freiburg (Schweiz) and Göttingen).

Naguib, S-A, *Le clergé féminin d'Amon thébain à la 21e dynastie*. Orientalia Lovaniensia Analecta 38 (Leuven 1990).

Naville, E, *The XIth dynasty temple at Deir el-Bahari*. 3 vols (London 1907-13).

Nelson, M, and Kalos, M, "Concessions funéraires du Moyen Empire découvertes au nord-ouest du Ramesseum," *Memnonia* 11 (2000), 131-51.

Nicholson, P T, and Shaw, I, *Ancient Egyptian Materials and Technologies* (Cambridge 2000).

Niwinski, A, "Ritual Protection of the Dead or Symbolic Reflection of his Special Status in Society? The Problem of the Black-coated Cartonnages and Coffins of the Third Intermediate Period," in Luft, E (ed.), *The Intellectual Heritage of Egypt. Studies presented to László Kákosy by Friends and Colleagues on the Occasion of his 60th Birthday*. Studia Aegyptiaca, 14 (Budapest 1992), 457-471.

Otto, E, *Das ägyptische Mundöffnungsritual*. 2 vols. Ägyptologische Abhandlungen 3 (Wiesbaden 1960).

Parkinson, R, *Cracking Codes. The Rosetta Stone and decipherment* (London 1999.

Parlasca, K, *Ritratti di Mummie*. 2 vols (Rome 1980).

Patch, D C, *Reflections of Greatness. Ancient Art at the Carnegie Museum of Natural History* (Pittsburg 1990).

Petrie, W M F, *Abydos*. 3 vols (London 1902-1904).

Petrie, W M F, *Gizeh and Rifeh* (London 1907).

Petrie, W M F, *Hawara, Biahmu and Arsinoë* (London 1889).

Petrie, W M F, *Kahun, Gurob and Hawara* (London 1890).

Porter, B, and Moss, R L B, assisted by E W Burney, *Topographical Bibliography of Ancient Egyptian Hieroglyphic Texts, Reliefs and Paintings*. 8 vols (Oxford 1927-99).

Quirke, S, and Spencer, A J, *The British Museum book of ancient Egypt* (London 1992).

Quirke, S, *Ancient Egyptian Religion* (London 1992).

Quirke, S, *Who Were the Pharaohs? A history of their names with a list of cartouches* (London 1990).

Quirke, S, *Owners of Funerary Papyri in the British Museum*. Occasional Paper 92 (London 1993).

Rammant-Peeters, A, *Les pyramidions égyptiens du Nouvel Empire*. Orientalia Lovaniensia Analecta 11 (Leuven 1983).

Raven, M J, "Corn-mummies," *Oudheidkundige Mededelingen uit het Rijksmuseum van Oudheden te Leiden* 63 (1982), 7-38.

Roberts, P C, " 'One of our Mummies is Missing': Evaluating Petrie's Records from Hawara," in Bierbrier, M L, (ed.), *Portraits and Masks. Burial Customs in Roman Egypt* (London 1997), 19-25.

Roth, A M, "The *psš-kf* and the 'Opening of the Mouth' Ceremony: A Ritual of Birth and Rebirth," *Journal of Egyptian Archaeology* 78 (1992), 113-47.

Sabbahy, L K, "The Titulary of the Harem of Nebhepetre Mentuhotep, Once Again," *Journal of the American Research Center in Egypt* 34 (1997), 163-6.

Schneider, H D, *Shabtis : an introduction to the history of ancient Egyptian funerary statuettes, with a catalogue of the collection of shabtis in the National Museum of Antiquities at Leiden.* 3 vols (Leiden 1977).

Seipel, W, *Ägypten. Götter, Gräber und die Kunst. 4000 Jahre Jenseitsglaube*. Exhibition Catalogue, Linz 1989 (Linz 1989).

Serpico, M, and White, R, "Resins, amber and bitumen," in Nicholson and Shaw (eds), *Ancient Egyptian Materials and Technologies*, 430-74.

Shaw, I, and Nicholson, P, *British Museum Dictionary of Ancient Egypt* (London 1995).

Sheikholeslami, C M, "The burials of priests of Montu at Deir el-Bahari in the Theban Necropolis," in Strudwick, N, and Taylor, J H, *The Theban Necropolis. Past, Present and Future* (London 2003), 131-7.

Silvano, F, "Le reticelle funerarie nell'Antico Egitto: proposte di interpretazione," *Egitto e vicino oriente* 3 (1980), 83-97.

Simpson, W K, *The Terrace of the Great God at Abydos: The Offering Chapels of Dynasties 12 and 13* (New Haven and Philadelphia 1974).

Sparks, R, "Egyptian stone vessels in Syro-Palestine during the Second Millennium B.C. and their impact on the local stone vessel industry," in Bunnens, G, (ed.), *Cultural Interaction in the Ancient Near East* (Louvain 1996).

Spencer, A J, *Death in Ancient Egypt* (Harmondsworth 1982).

Spencer, A J, *Early Dynastic Objects*. Catalogue of Egyptian Antiquities in the British Museum, 5 (London 1980).

Stead, M, *Egyptian life* (London 1986).

Stocks, D, *Experiments in Egyptian* Archaeology (London and New York 2003).

Taylor, J H, "Masks in Ancient Egypt. The Image of divinity," in Mack, J, *Masks. The Art of Expression* (London 1994), 168-89.

Taylor, J H, "Patterns of colouring on ancient Egyptian coffins from the New Kingdom to the Twenty-sixth dynasty: an overview," in Davies, W V, (ed.), *Colour and Painting in Ancient Egypt* (London 2001), 164-81.

Taylor, J H, "Theban coffins during the Twenty-second to the Twenty-sixth dynasty: dating and synthesis of development," in Strudwick, N, and Taylor, J H, *The Theban Necropolis. Past, Present and Future* (London 2003), 95-121.

Taylor, J H, *Death and the afterlife in Ancient Egypt* (London 2001).

Taylor, J H, *Mummy: the inside story* (London 2004).

Vandier, J, *Tombes de Deir el-Médineh : la tombe de Nefer-Abou.* Mémoires publiés par les membres de l'Institut français d'archéologie orientale 69 (Cairo 1935).

Walker, S, and Bierbrier, M, *Ancient Faces. Mummy Portraits from Roman Egypt.* Exhibition Catalogue, London 1997 (London 1997).

Wilkinson, R H, *The complete Gods and Goddesses of Ancient Egypt* (London 2003).

Willems, H, *Chests of Life. A Study of the Typology and Conceptual Development of Middle Kingdom Standard Class Coffins* (Leiden 1988).

Wilson, P, "Sais and its secrets," *Egyptian Archaeology* 18 (2001), 3-5.

Yoyotte, J, "Une monumentale litanie de granit: les Sekhmet d'Aménophis III et la conjuration permanente de la déesse dangereuse," *Bulletin de la société française d'Egyptologie* 87-88 (1980), 47-75.

Ziegler, C, (ed.), *The Pharaohs.* Exhibition Catalogue, Venice 2002 (Milan 2002).

Zivie-Coche, C M, *Giza au premier millénaire. Autour du temple d'Isis Dame des Pyramides* (Boston 1991).